MAPPING

IN THE AGE OF
DIGITAL MEDIA

MAPPING

IN THE AGE OF DIGITAL MEDIA

The Yale Symposium

Mike Silver and Diana Balmori

⟨W⟩ WILEY-ACADEMY

Cover: Detail of flow animations (movie stills), Mike Silver.

Published in Great Britain in 2003 by Wiley-Academy, a division of John Wiley & Sons Ltd

Copyright © 2003 John Wiley & Sons Ltd,

The Atrium, Southern Gate, Chichester, West Sussex PO19 8SQ, United Kingdom

Telephone   (+44) 1243 779777

Email (for orders and customer service enquiries): cs-books@wiley.co.uk

Visit our Home Page on www.wileyeurope.com or www.wiley.com

This publication is designed to provide accurate and authoritative information in regard to the subject matter covered. It is sold on the understanding that the Publisher is not engaged in rendering professional services. If professional advice or other expert assistance is required, the services of a competent professional should be sought.

Other Wiley Editorial Offices

John Wiley & Sons Inc., 111 River Street, Hoboken, NJ 07030, USA

Jossey-Bass, 989 Market Street, San Francisco, CA 94103-1741, USA

Wiley-VCH Verlag GmbH, Boschstr. 12, D-69469 Weinheim, Germany

John Wiley & Sons Australia Ltd, 33 Park Road, Milton, Queensland 4064, Australia

John Wiley & Sons (Asia) Pte Ltd, 2 Clementi Loop #02-01, Jin Xing Distripark, Singapore 129809

John Wiley & Sons Canada Ltd, 22 Worcester Road, Etobicoke, Ontario, Canada M9W 1L1

ISBN 0470-85076-0

Design and Prepress: ARTMEDIAPRESS Ltd, London

Printed and bound in Italy

Contents

Acknowledgements

This book grew out of a day-long symposium held at the Yale School of Architecture in the spring of 2002. It is both a record of presentations made by different scientists, artists, designers, geographers and theorists as well as an elaboration on their ideas, since a few of the contributing individuals were not present at the initial gathering.

Mapping in the Age of Digital Media is a trans-disciplinary survey of new computer-based mapping technologies. While the authors explore different terrain, their writings on the whole demonstrate a shared interest in complex phenomenon, a critical attitude towards new media tools, and a practical interest in applied mapping techniques mixed with an insistent desire to find new ways of working.

Aside from the introductory texts and conclusion, the book has been divided into three sections. The first focuses on the mapping of surfaces ('Skins and Walls'), the second examines time and movement ('Mapping Time'), while the third ('Below the Surface') explores the deep space extending beneath the skins of objects, living bodies and landscapes. This last section explores the inevitable increase of computing power by examining high-resolution maps, voxel modeling and supercomputer simulations. In this sense the volume represents a bridge that joins current technologies with things to come.

In the process of assembling the book, many individuals made important contributions to both the projects and the texts. I am deeply grateful for the dedication and work of my co-editor Diana Balmori, whose persistence and insight have been of immeasurable value. A tremendous sense of appreciation must also be extended to Jennifer Castellon, Jean Sielaff, Rob Liston, Daniel Staffieri and John Jacobson who helped organize the symposium. For editing, reviews and suggestions for the text, I would like to express my sincere gratitude to John Beckmann, Harlan Brothers, Peng Chia, Nina Rappaport, Abigail Grater and the staff at Wiley-Academy, Caroline Ellerby, Paul Butkus, Benoit Mandelbrot, Jeff Kipnis for his encouraging review at Ohio State, and Keller Easterling for her unflagging support at Yale. I am also thankful for the work done by Hiro Shimizu, Sam Rosenthal, Ryan Minney, J C Nelson, David Serrero (VRML Simulator 1) and Jaehuk Choi at my office, and for the corporate support of Cyra Inc, William Deitz and John Stienhoff of Flow Analysis Inc, Chris Roquefort of Inspec Inc, James E Palhel from Land Mapping Services and Dean Barr of Croma North America. Howard Lefevre, Robert Livsey and the staff at Ohio State's Knowlton School of Architecture were also instrumental in the support of research that led to the completion of this book. I would also like to thank Karen Van Lengen, Mark Tsurumaki, Joel Sanders and Peter Wheelright at the Parsons School of Design where I was first able to explore the subject of digital mapping in a semester-long lecture series entitled 'Informed Terrain'.

For the invaluable opportunity to share new ideas I would of course like to thank the writers, artists and scientists who participated in the projects. Finally, both the book and symposium would not have been possible without the generous support of Alexandro Gehry, Frank O Gehry, Dean Robert A M Stern and the Graham Foundation for the Advancement of the Arts.

Mike Silver

PREFACE

The Yale School of Architecture Symposium on Digital Mapping, held in April 2002, addressed a field that is new not only to music, film, art, science and cultural geography but also to architecture and urbanism. The digital capabilities that now enable us visually to document and dissect various forms, materials and structures both above and below the surface of the body, the earth and the city, offer new possibilities for understanding and designing the relationship between the natural and the man-made world.

This thought-provoking collection of essays, interviews and images highlights the diverse opportunities that flourish under the umbrella of digital mapping in a trans-disciplinary exchange. At Yale, digital mapping is now one of the many technologies students can harness in conjunction with, and parallel to, the traditional tools of pencil and paper, in developing their individual visual expression.

We look forward to the more nuanced architecture and urbanism that the interaction between the physical and the virtual world promises.

Robert A M Stern
Dean, Yale School of Architecture

INTRODUCTION
Mapping in the Age of Digital Media

Mike Silver

'The process takes approximately 17 seconds … The subject should be as relaxed as possible in order to reduce his heart rate. A strong rapid pulse will appear in the raw scan as a series of vertical ridges spaced across the base of the throat … the data gets smeared.'

Doug Kelly, *Character Animation in Depth*, 1998[1]

In *The Man Who Mistook His Wife for a Hat*, Oliver Sacks describes a neurological disorder that impairs the ability of its victims to recognize faces, landscapes and other complex phenomena. One of Sacks's patients (a music teacher) was condemned by this dysfunction to experience the world as an unending series of abstractions. When asked to identify a glove, the patient became perplexed. He was, it seems, unable to recognize objects in relationship to the network of memories, social customs and experiences that place things in context. Instead what he saw was 'a continuous surface … infolded on itself … useful perhaps as a change purse … for coins of five sizes'.[2] The patient had little difficulty naming the platonic

Unfolded mesh taken from a 3-D scan of the face.

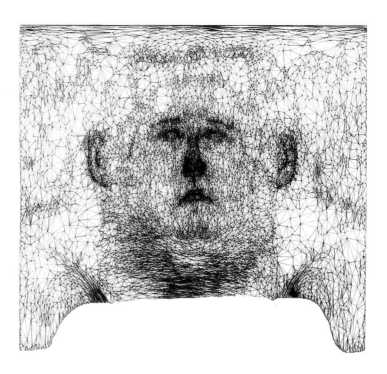

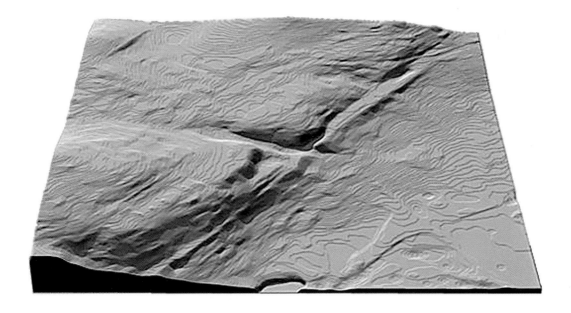

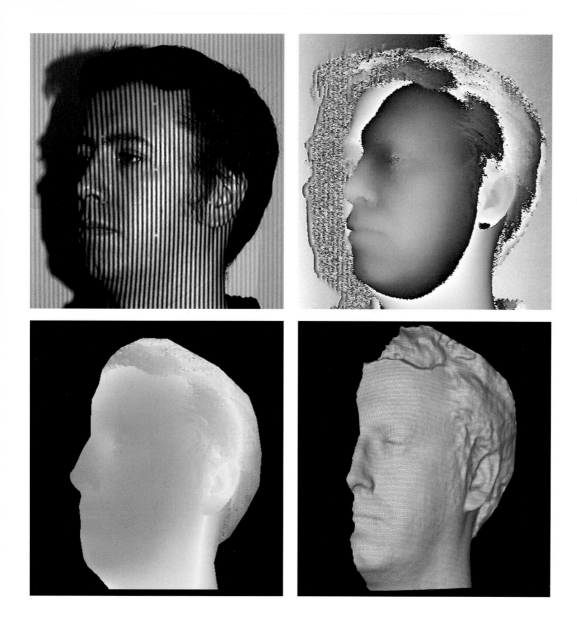

solids from a kit of shapes Sacks kept as a diagnostic tool, but when it came to people, their expressions and the concrete realities of appearance the patient was lost – sometimes mistaking animate forms for inanimate ones.

Individuals with this disorder apparently manage their day-to-day social interactions by taking cues from a simple taxonomy of features – a mole, a birthmark or the silhouette traced by the clean geometry of a person's hairline. Reduced to simple features, what escapes this 'visual agnosia' is the overall being or identity characterized by complex and nuanced gestures. Patients exhibit 'an almost Picasso-like power to see, and equally depict … organizations embedded in, and normally lost in the concrete'.[3] While such an impairment can serve to parody the shortcomings of Modernism's prolonged obsession with reductivist theories of form, it also points to the 'ineluctable modality of the visible'[4] in a complex and irreducible world.

OPPOSITE:
**Inspec Inc's moiré phase-shifting
process calculates spatial depth
using projected grids and interpolation algorithms.**

With the invention of standardized mass-production techniques and the wide-spread changes brought about by the Industrial Revolution, abstraction in the arts prevailed. Prohibitions on the use of ornament were aesthetically formulated, non-figurative painting was born from changes effected by the invention of photography – and the machine aesthetic took hold. In these examples the historical development of abstraction can be traced directly to the rapid acceleration of technological change. And yet, in today's world of computer networks and information technology we are already beginning to see a paradigmatic shift away from the 'general' towards modes of apprehending the world that are more specifically concrete.

In recent years, new digital-mapping technologies have begun profoundly to alter the ways we measure and represent space. These techniques operate at multiple scales – from the global to the local – and are employed in a variety of disciplines from geology to the biological sciences: 3-D scanning technology, advanced laser altimetry and magnetic resonance imaging (MRI) to mention just a few, have produced unique images of the body and its terrestrial environment.

Mapping in ways not reduced to generalized schemes underscores the complex nature of processes and phenomena that are impossible to record using conventional techniques. Improvements in our ability to predict the weather or map the human genome are as much dependent on enhanced computational power as they are on newer and more sophisticated systems of data acquisition.

In these examples new mapping tools form a crucial link in the chain of data processing where nature, information and material culture become intertwined. But can the real be understood exclusively in these terms? If the answer is no, then it is because the alliance of physical space and data space has become far too volatile. Defined as such, the real is a force without measure or certainty; attempt to manage it evade even the best plans.

This fact was ingeniously summed up in *Looker* the low-budget science-fiction thriller written by Michael Crichton in 1981. Crichton's narrative hinged on the virtual reproduction of fashion models that were digitally recorded and then killed. This move to control the female body by replacing it with a computer-generated substitute relies for its poignancy on an ever-increasing technical mastery and on the possibility of creating extremely deceptive simulations. And yet even in this film the power of feminine desire returns in a narrative haunted by the technocratic male gaze – a gaze threatened by a volition and will existing outside its own (Freud's castration anxiety).

Like *The Stepford Wives*, *Looker* is a parody of contemporary technocultural attempts to control the uncertainties of everyday life. As part of a murderous

conspiracy, the scanners in the film produce copies without referents or hyper-realities. The synthetic actress/models generated from these maps are indistin-guishable (at least on TV) from a reality that once existed but no longer breathes. An assemblage of data therefore becomes the perfect surrogate form.

These artificial women, capable of performing (unpaid) the endless tasks assigned to them, become the ultimate advertising medium – the women they re-present are both robotic simulations and carefully manipulated signs. Here control implies mediation as an extension of knowledge and power, and yet in *Looker* Crichton ingeniously demonstrates the futility of this kind of technological domination by defining the real as the very thing that escapes representation.

Notes
1 Doug Kelly, *Character Animation in Depth*, The Coriolis Group (Scottsdale, Arizona), 1998.
2 Oliver Sacks, *The Man Who Mistook His Wife for a Hat*, Touchstone Books (New York),1998, p 15.
3 Ibid, p 18.
4 James Joyce, *Ulysses*, Vintage Books (New York), 1986, p 31.

JUST IN TIME

Diana Balmori

Sometime in the 1960s, mapping changed, as did its discipline geography. The new work went beyond traditional notions of cartography, from the static drawings of the earth's surface to dynamic maps of human activity that had to be updated every year – think of the political boundaries in Africa since the 1960s.

Geographer Carl Sauer's work *The Early Spanish Main* (1966)[1] exemplifies this change. Sauer's picture of the early Caribbean as the Spanish found it when they reached America was a picture not of a frozen geography but one where various native human groups exchanged plants, building techniques, tools and words over an area covering many islands. Sauer's work and Berkeley's School of Historical Geography, as it came to be called, surfaced nationally in the 1970s. However, antecedents to these developments included *French Annales*, a historical geography journal first published in Paris in 1946, and George Marsh's *Physical Geography as Modified by Human Action*,[2] which was ignored at the time of its surprisingly early publication in 1867 though later rediscovered and acclaimed in the 1960s (Marsh was the founder of Yale's School of Forestry and Environmental Studies).

As it transformed mapping, historical geography also transformed academic geography. In some departments, geography became absorbed into history, changed its name to historical geography in others (UCLA) or was phased out altogether (Yale).

Hispaniola: native province and subdivisions.

The Making of the English Landscape (1955)[3] by the English geographer W G Hoskins, and *Design with Nature* (1969)[4] by landscape architect Ian McHarg, were important works on the human modification of their respective landscapes. For example, McHarg's text overlaid maps of physical geography with information from very different sources – historical, statistical and urbanistic, and these map overlays, printed on clear plastic, led directly to geographical information systems (GIS). With the appearance of GIS as the main mapping tool came the institutional demise of physical geography and the emergence of the short-lived, constantly changing maps of historical geography.

Short-lived maps, however, are also the result of technological developments in the late twentieth century that made map-printing easy and inexpensive. Thus though the idea of adding human activity to the physical geography had emerged in the nineteenth century, it had no effect on mapping as it was not economically feasible to produce constantly updated maps. Marsh's book had to wait a whole century before it would have an impact.

Human activity was considered artificial in the nineteenth century. However, the new maps made the areas of 'human' and 'the natural' overlap and blur. If human artifacts are designated as part of a landscape, the validity of the division comes into question.

Compared to the slow pace of geological change, the rapidly shifting pace of human history made it possible to capture physical events such as floods, volcanic eruptions and hurricanes moving up the coast that could not be recorded using traditional means. New technologies are more fluid, time being the new dimension of mapping. Where only space was mapped before, we are now mapping time, the next step being the recording of events as they happen (stills become animations; photographs become motion pictures). The closest we have come to this so far was demonstrated during the attacks on the World Trade Center when 2,600 maps showing the changing conditions in the area around Ground Zero were produced over a three-month period (see 'Networking Maps: GIS, Virtualized Reality and the World Wide Web', pp 48–55).

Another way of putting this is that current mapping techniques have a much greater temporal resolution. These maps allow us to catch ephemera before they are missed completely. What is more, reality is transformed by these frequent observations, as shown in the examples below.

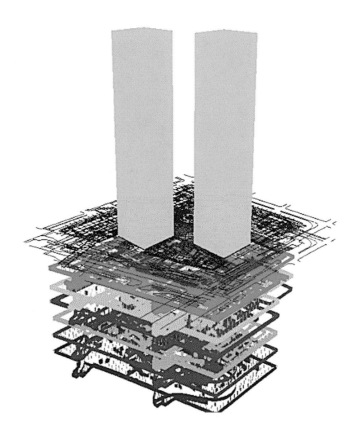

GIS maps of the World Trade Center.

1 Measurements of phosphorus in urban streams monitored once a month versus urban streams monitored in 15-minute intervals yielded a completely different picture. Phosphorus appeared in negligible quantities in the first case and in large quantities in peaks that went off the chart in the second. Since phosphorus is deleterious to the biota of rivers, the data led to a plan for action where none was needed before.[5]

2 Glaucoma has been detected by measuring pressure in the eye. During continuous monitoring, peaks of pressure were discovered while patients slept, overturning earlier understanding of what causes the disorder. This continuous surveillance allowed for a record of much finer detail.[6]

3 The analysis of blood glucose levels in diabetics produced a different picture when continuous 48-hour monitoring was used in place of periodic checks.[7]

Physical geography has been able to produce very detailed spatial maps, but only recently has it developed methods to record rapid changes over time (in reverse the course image-resolution of certain neuroscientific instruments is compensated by their ability to detect instantaneous changes). Focusing on time at a much finer resolution captures changes before unnoticed yielding images of a reality that is in constant flux, where the static, solid matter of our world melts into a series of temporary events.

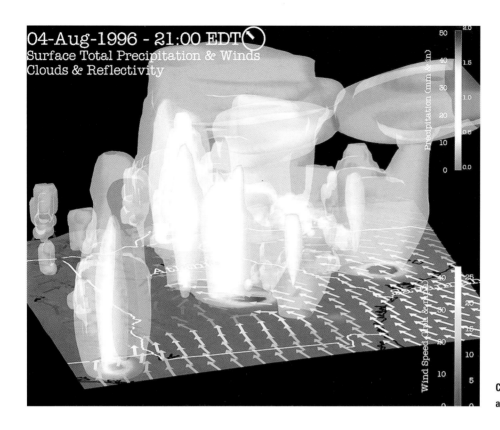

04-Aug-1996 - 21:00 EDT
Surface Total Precipitation & Winds
Clouds & Reflectivity

**Computer simulation of the
atmosphere over Atlanta, 1996.**

Notes

1 Carl Ortwin Sauer, *The Early Spanish Main*, University of California Press (Berkeley, Cal), 1966.

2 George P Marsh, *Man and Nature or Physical Geography as Modified by Human Action*, Charles Scribner & Co (Broadway, New York), 1867.

3 W G Hoskins, *The Making of the English Landscape*, Hodder & Stoughton (London), 1992, first printed 1955.

4 Ian L McHarg, *Design with Nature*, Natural History Press (New York), 1969.

5 A Cattaneo and Y T Prairie, 'Temporal variability in the chemical characteristics along the Riviere De Lachigan: How many samples are necessary to describe stream chemistry?', *Canadian Journal of Fisheries and Aquatic Sciences* 52(4), April 1995, pp 828–35, and J H Lee, K W Bang, L H Ketchum, J S Cho and M J Yu, 'First flush analysis of urban storm runoff', *Science of the Total Environment* 293(1–3), 3 July 2002, pp 163–75.

6 Moderator: Martin B Wax, MD (Chair), Faculty: Carl B Camras, MD, Richard G Fiscella, RPH, MPH, Christopher Girkin, MD, Kuldev Singh, MD, and Robert N Weinreb, MD, 'Emerging perspectives in glaucoma: Optimizing 24-hour control of intraocular pressure', *American Journal of Ophthalmology*, Vol 133, No 6, June 2002.

7 George D Molnar, MD, Division of Endocrinology, Department of Internal Medicine, William F Taylor, PhD, Department of Medical Statistics and Epidemiology and Alice L Langworthy, 'Plasma immuno-reactive insulin patterns in insulin-treated diabetics: Studies during continuous blood glucose monitoring', *Section of Medical Statistics: Mayo Clinic Proceedings*, Vol 47, October 1972, Rochester, Minnesota.

Games, Mapping and Mediation

Branden Hookway

Mapping and simulation

The growing importance of mapping – not only in techniques of visualization but in the political economy itself – can be traced to advances in scanning technologies and the use of the computer as a data-management tool. These advances have enhanced the power of maps as a technique for storing, prioritizing and presenting data. As reflected in the work assembled for this publication, digital mapping encompasses many different practices and techniques, ranging from art and architecture to urban planning and disaster response, and from medicine and physics to land use and surveillance. Behind these different applications lie common traits that point to the use of maps within a larger socio-technical system: an assemblage of technologies and organizational strategies dedicated to the modeling of a given environment, to the extent that it allows and encourages certain critical decision-making with regard to that environment, as defined by the system itself.

If we are to understand the contemporary use of mapping, we cannot, then, consider it either as a purely visual technique or as rooted within one particular discipline. Rather we must look to those systems within which mapping operates as constituent techniques. These systems, which could be said to operate according to the rules of a game, represent the general organizational dynamic at work in contemporary society.

This is not to deny the purely visual power of mapping. Mapping is a form of control in that it determines what is seen and how it is seen. However, digital and cybernetic technologies have amplified the strategic value of mapping precisely by extending it into the realm of the computational. If the control system theorized by Foucault could be described as a 'system of light',[1] which operates through the act of rendering the previously hidden visible, contemporary techniques of control have passed far beyond the visual spectrum and even beyond the range of the (augmented) human eye. If visualization retains power in the contemporary world, or perhaps even power over the world, it is only to the extent that it is computational as well, in effect transforming the world into so much source material to be scanned at ever greater resolutions, translated into larger and more inclusive sets of data, and analyzed and cross-referenced by ever more powerful analytical and design tools. Foucault's 'systems of light' now extend to the limits of the electromagnetic spectrum, with resolution approaching that of a single electron, and

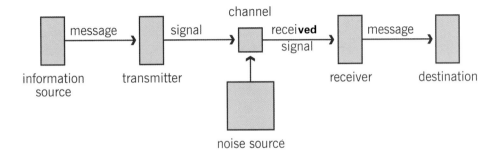

Figure 1: Claude Shannon's schematic diagram of a general communication system.

perhaps most significantly a complexity capable of self-organization and intelligence.

The map has always been an instrument for strategic decision-making. Its predictive power has only been enhanced with the advent of digital mapping. The map has now become the site upon which a logic of simulation works to model increasingly complex environments with a greater degree of accuracy. A simulation produces within itself a map of a given external environment, complete with the modeled functionality of that environment. Within a simulation, different courses of action can be played out in order to determine the possible result of those actions in the external environment. Different strategies or tactics may be developed, tried out and even practiced.

While it has always been intended that maps be viewed strategically, the subsumption of the map within the simulation has led to a whole new state of affairs. As complex environments in the world are increasingly subjected to control through modeling and simulation, we interact with the world through increasingly complex mediations. Everything – from bodies to economies and from molecules to cities – may be mapped, simulated and tested. Everything becomes subject to the logic of a game.

Information diagrams

For Claude Shannon, in his well-known structural diagram of a general system of information transmission (1948)[2] (Figure 1) and for information theory in general, the critical issue is that the message be identical in content (exactly or approximately) at each side of the diagram: at both its input into the transmitter and at its output from the receiver. Every step in between is a potential disruption of the message.

As can be seen in Figure 1, Shannon was most concerned with the effects of noise on a signal as it travels from transmitter to receiver. Information theory was designed to seek out the various ways a given message, now understood as information, could be coded so as to travel the gauntlet through transmitter, channel and receiver, to emerge largely unscathed at the other side of a communication system.

The concept of information includes not only content but also a protocol of communication, for the most part viewed by information theory as neutral to, or outside, the meaning it conveys. Information theory allows us to abstract information from its specific content, in order to study how a given communication protocol can best navigate a given system of transmission. This insight – that information possesses its own operational rules regardless of content – is exceptionally powerful. In its application to many disciplines, information has in itself driven the convergence of all disciplines around shared techniques of data management. Information theory itself was an outgrowth of work on cybernetics, which conceived of biological and technological systems alike as involving the transmission and reception of signals. Today it seems that any advance in techniques of information manipulation, whether in art or in science, can and will find an application outside of its field of origin.

Information theory finds its greatest realization in the computer, which has had a powerful synthetic effect in transforming discipline-specific forms of knowledge – captured through some mode of scanning – into abstract and mutually compatible information. The computer has only increased the rate of transfer of technologies and techniques across disciplines, allowing advances in one field to be quickly applied to another. For example, both MRI medical imaging and subsurface visualization of the earth's crust for oil exploration make use of voxel (or 3-D pixel) modeling technology, and a significant advance in voxel modeling, achieved perhaps in first-person shooter computer-gaming, would certainly find an application in these two fields.

Information theory is mostly unconcerned with the mediation effects of information. Yet information itself is a form of mediation, or even a medium, in that it transforms source material and meaning into a form compatible with a given communication protocol. We cannot then consider the content of information, and by extension that of contemporary media or mapping techniques, without considering its mediated state. In becoming information, content is essentially bound to the mechanics of mediation.

Mediation diagrams

Mediation – and here I refer to any medium or media, regardless of its aims, field of operation or technical standard – digital, analog or otherwise – must involve at the very least the capture of some form of source material, the translation of the captured material into a form compatible with transmission, and the transmission of this material to a receiver. This process could be diagrammed as shown in Figure 2.

Each of the three steps entails a qualitative change in the source material itself. Each assigns to its input material a format or system of rules that accrues to that material, to determine the way the source material is to function within a given socio-technical system. This process of formatting could be termed the protocol of a given form of mediation. Any source material undergoing mediation, then,

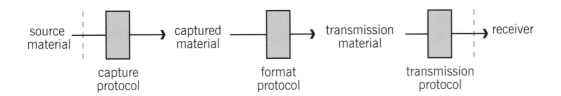

source material → capture protocol → captured material → format protocol → transmission material → transmission protocol → receiver

Figure 2: Mediation diagram 1.

will then assume the protocol of a given medium merely through the act of its capture and transmission by means of that medium. By taking on media protocol as a fundamental quality, raw source material is transformed into a media object, in that it is now formatted for media use and carries within itself the utilities of capture and transmission.

The mediation diagram in Figure 2 is of course a simplification in a number of ways, not least in that it models only a one-way process: a straight line from source material to receiver. We can imagine this as the simple translation of a landscape into a painting, a film or a map, as received by a viewer. Yet the various and complex effects of mediation upon culture, and of culture upon mediation, suggest that we should be able to move through the diagram in any number of ways. For example, economic factors have often driven the development of forms and technologies of mediation, based in no small part on the reactions or feedback from receivers (the audience, users, etc), which would throw the diagram into reverse.

Certainly other examples of feedback exist as well. Any kind of refinement of mediation techniques will involve some sort of feedback mechanism, in effect allowing mediation protocols to test by themselves their own effectiveness. A classic technological model of this can be found in cybernetics. In radar (radio direction and ranging) or the more recent laser-based technology of light direction and ranging (LIDAR), energy is transmitted into an environment, and its reflection then captured and analyzed. Here, the radar operator, in the position of the receiver, could be seen as sending information backwards through the diagram towards the source material, which would then reflect it through a different yet systemically linked technological protocol back to the operator. The relative simplicity of the radar operator's interface belies the complexity of the information path between interface and scanned environment, and the number of acts of translation that must occur along the way.

In Figure 2, then, each of these one-way processes can be seen as both reciprocal and iterative. We can imagine captured material feeding backwards to affect the source material itself, just as we can imagine the receiver (spectator, etc) acting upon the transmitted material, and thereby altering it. This has the overall effect of drawing both the source material and the receiver into the set of relationships defined by media protocol in the course of mediation, complicating attempts to conceive of either the source material or the receiver outside of its influence.

We can further complicate the diagram by considering the role of intentionality or authorship, whether as a conscious or inadvertent act, in mediation. Transmitted material may be shaped with respect to its meaning, content or form at any point along the mediation diagram. In film, for example, the source material, that which

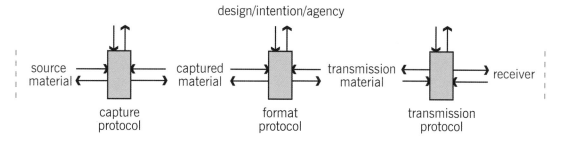

Figure 3: Mediation diagram 2.

is filmed, may be chosen, arranged, framed or rehearsed; the format, camera, lens, focus and camera path chosen; the film-stock tinted, toned, reformatted or digitized; the film cut and spliced; words, images and filmed or digital content inserted directly into the frame and so on. Similar inputs can be found in other media such as painting or military war-games: in short, in any technique of mediation.

At the same time, we should also imagine the feedback mechanisms discussed above applying to intentionality in mediation. Again this is likely obvious as intentional decisions themselves must be reconciled with the source material at hand and to the range of choices available with a given protocol of mediation. Indeed, the greater the complexity of a given system of mediation, the greater the number of possible contact points for feedback between that system and intentionality, and the more that intentionality must be moderated by the protocols of mediation. A modified diagram might look like that shown in Figure 3.

Information increases the speed of this process only by bringing together in a single action (or mediation) the capture, formatting and transmission of material. This removes crucial friction associated with moving between different protocols, and leads to a seamless appearance of transparent mediation. Our diagram could then be simplified to that shown in Figure 4.

Some form of protocol stands between every interaction of intentionality (as in that of a designer) with the world, the work and the work's audience. In the movement through these diagrams, each step involves some form of transaction, whether as a mediation or as a decision. With the growing complexity of media and the growing mediation of complexity, the pathway through this diagram becomes itself more complex, even as it appears more seamless, more transparent.

The rules of the game

The game is ultimately active and does not admit to the implied passivity of the spectator or the spectacle, except as one model within a range of possible choices. This is a particularly important distinction today as social production has come to rely almost completely on an economy of decision-making. Decisions, ranging from transactions to the production of ideas and their implementation in society, have become the economic lifeblood of society, with various forms of technological mediation acting as the circulation system. The rules of the game by which the decisions of individuals and groups are coordinated at a social level are for the most part determined by a socio-technical system encompassing the forms of technological mediation along with the social organizations that have evolved with them. The reliance upon rules of the game allows market logic to expand in all directions,

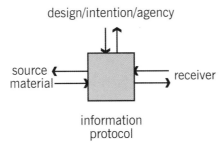

tying together seamlessly the global economy with the economies of attention, of which the spectacle is only one constituent part.

Mediation serves the game by processing the world as a data set, or map, accessible to the rules of the game. Mediation occurs repeatedly during the course of the game and at many different points within the game structure. It includes all processes of scanning or capturing input from the world, whether in what could be termed game design or the creation of the data set that will serve as the game environment, or in game play or the manipulation of that game environment. Every interaction between the game environment and the world is an act of mediation – from the action of a film camera or image-editing software, or an MRI scanner or satellite GIS imaging, to the manipulation of that environment by a user, such as a scientist, designer, spectator or gamer. The general mechanisms of mediation thus extend beyond the usual definitions of media as limited to cultural phenomena, to include the natural and social sciences, as in the exploration of natural resources, demographic studies, market research, war games and the like. In short, mediation occurs in any field that makes use of virtual environments.

Game environments (see Figure 5) are both spatial and temporal. In the first case, mediation produces a data environment that can possess elements existing simultaneously and in relation to one another, and that could potentially be measured by those qualities pertaining to space, such as relative distance. In the second case, the environment possesses its own time frame, which may or may not model 'real time'. Game time may also be subjected to any number of temporal operations, such as being played backwards, repeated or frozen in time. In the course of game play, a user can expect to interact with the game environment both spatially and temporally. The game environment is designed to function in relation to the user's decision-making (in terms of speed of decision-making, pattern recognition, cognitive ability, reasoning etc), and should be seen as codependent with the cognition of the user. Thus the evolution of game environments seems to carry out its own program of scanning, measuring and training human cognitive potential.

Game environments are always linked through mediation to 'real' environments, although this linkage takes different forms. The market itself provides a model of a game environment where the myriad simultaneous acts of mediation occur in such a way as to seemingly erase any distinction between the game and the real. We can imagine that this would be the case in human cognition as well, with consciousness as a process of mediation between neural activity and cultural training. Like neural networks, which generate complex behaviors through the action of billions of neurons acting in parallel, so the market harnesses myriad transactions,

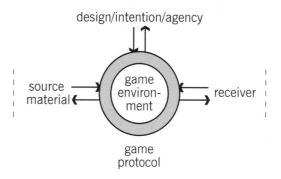

Figure 5: Mediation diagram 4.

each the result of a series of decisions at the individual or group level, to produce economic expansion and growth. Our current fascination with these self-regulating systems is in many ways the result of the growing complexity and sophistication of technologically mediated game environments, which for the first time allow the insertion of social control into processes that were previously considered complex beyond human understanding. Human organizations can now take on far more complex forms than in the past, leading, for example, to the decline of less efficient centralized-control hierarchies associated with the state, and the growing power of economies as a political force.

Just as the spectacle is no longer purely passive in the society of the game, so consumption can no longer be seen as a passive event. Consumption is of course aligned with production but not in the sense of a negative quantity that must be balanced with its positive. It is aligned with production in that it takes part in the act of production itself, so that the act of consumption registers only as a positive quantity: the addition of a single decision into a social decision matrix, as in the choice to consume a specific commodity. This serves to further blur distinctions between classes or at least to force us to look at the ways decisions are made in society at every level – the ways decisions are encoded within society, who makes what kinds of decisions and how they are filtered through society – if we are to understand the relationship of individuals, groups or classes to the functioning of political economy.

Mediation, which always seeks to be frictionless, sets itself against those elements or practices that would resist its potential expansion. Resistance is as essential for mediation as it is for an electronic circuit, as though mediation requires ever expanding boundaries. The sources of resistance can be cultural, social, technological and even biological. Each of these serves as a problematic and demands of mediation a response, but it is the wetware of the human central nervous system that continues to prove to be both the fundamental limit of mediation and its eventual prize. Mapping, then, serves as a form of capture, making available previously unmediated environments to the predations of a game economy.

Notes
1 Gilles Deleuze, *Foucault*, University of Minnesota Press (Minneapolis),1988, p 32.
2 See C E Shannon, 'A mathematical theory of communication',*The Bell System Technical Journal*, Vol 27, July 1948, pp 379–81.

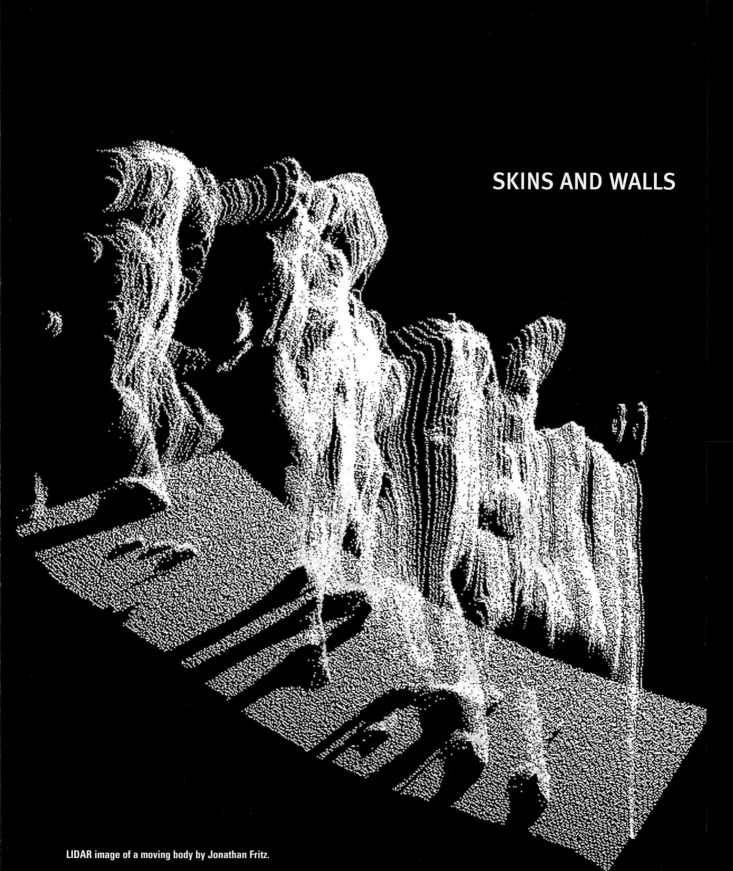

SKINS AND WALLS

LIDAR image of a moving body by Jonathan Fritz.

'Essay of a Thousand Layers' (still image from animation), 2002.

BODIES UNFOLDING

selfportrait.map

Lilla LoCurto and Bill Outcault

After seeing Buckminster Fuller's 'Dymaxion World Map', a projection of the earth as a flattened isohedron, we began working on the idea of using computer technology to transfer the details of our physical bodies onto two-dimensional surfaces. Representing 3-D objects on two-dimensional surfaces has been a concern for artists through the centuries, and the concept of simultaneity where all views of an object are experienced at once was a major theme of the Cubists and Futurists. We conceived 'selfportrait.map' to explore this in a contemporary way using new digital-imaging tools.

The earliest map projections were produced by first visually and later mathematically projecting 3-D details onto two-dimensional surfaces. With the advent of computers, ever more complex objects could be electronically recorded and transformed. As artists accustomed to working with physical materials like clay, stone or steel, we considered the manipulation of 3-D forms in virtual space, like map projections, as a non-traditional extension of the sculptural process.

Selfportrait.map looks at the digital reordering of 3-D forms through a reshaping of the digitized body and offers an alternative way of representing the human figure by remapping its surface onto a set of simple shapes. The fragility and tenuous nature of existence is a recurring theme in our work, and in the process of unfolding the scans the computer generated a complex network of jagged seams and torn edges. Although stitching utilities exist that allow the projections to be repaired, we considered the holes and gaps to be evocative of both landscape maps and fragile skins.

The scanner we used consisted of four recording heads mounted on vertical tracks that surround a stage where the subject is scanned from the top down. The device uses both lasers and digital cameras which produce files containing photographic data tied to spatial coordinates. In order to create maps of the scan data we used the Geocart cartography software and software written with a mathematician that enabled Geocart to import our figures as databases.

The scanner's software also contains a utility program to align the four cameras, and this creates horizontally oriented topographic sections. Likewise, we used our software, augmented to allow more manipulation of the model, and sectioned our scanned bodies into innumerable slices. As each layer was separated from the next it could be viewed as an individual drawing, and by varying the depth and position

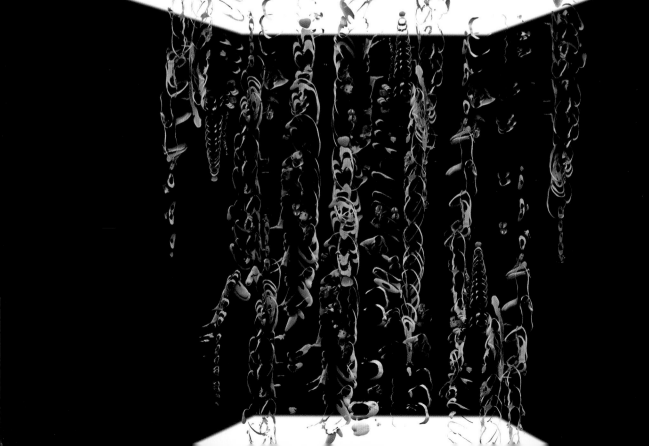

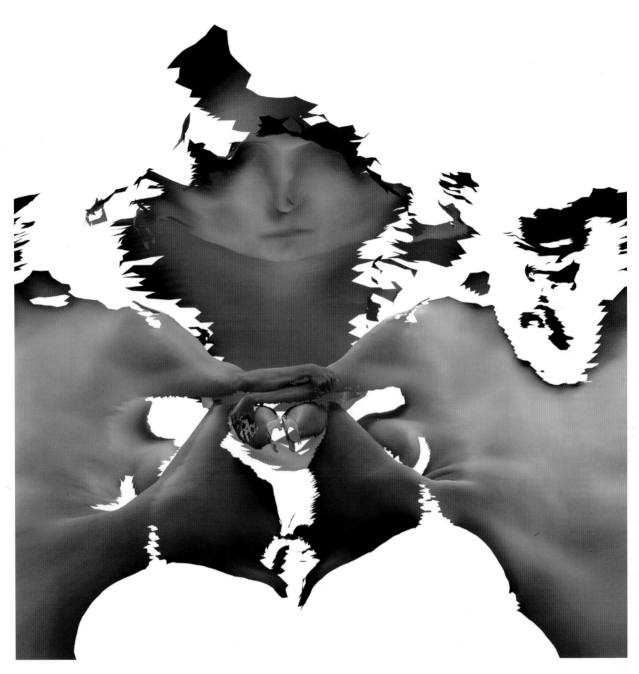

Adams World in a Square 1 L3sph(8/6) 7_98, chromogenic print, 2000.

OPPOSITE:
'Essay of a Thousand Layers' (still image from animation), 2002.

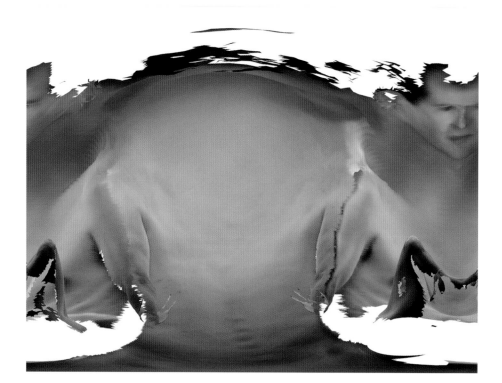

Gall Stereographic
BClsph(8/6)7_98, chromogenic
print, 2000.

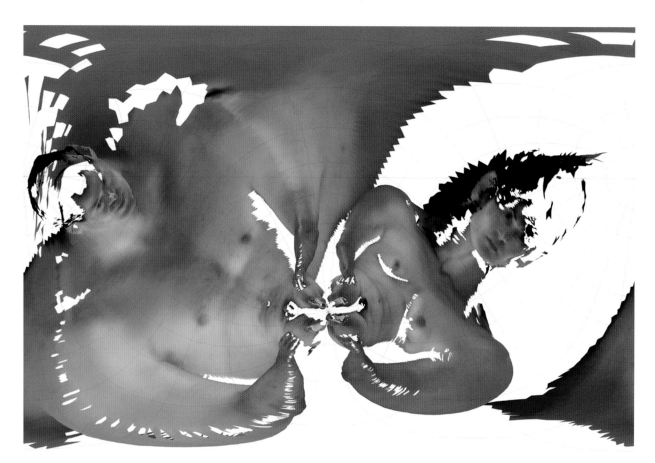

BSAM BL1sph(8/7)7_98, chromogenic print, 2000.

Conformal Lagrange L2sph(8/6)7_98, inkjet print, 2001.

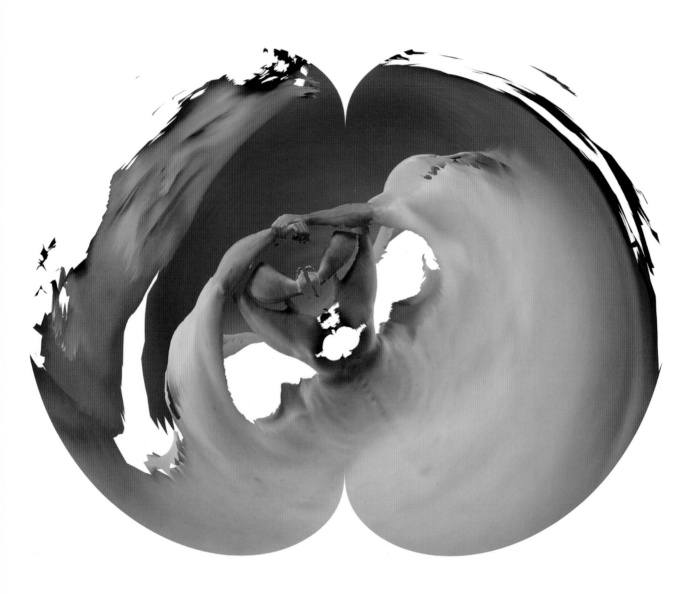

Polyconic BS1sph(8/6)7_98, chromogenic print, 2000.

of each slice a complex, painterly set of calligraphic lines that resemble brush-strokes was developed.

From compilations of these sections we created a short animation. Imagine look-ing down at a topographic map, seeing only the topmost layer and then scanning through each stratum, one layer at a time. Altering the angle and depth of each stratum greatly affects the appearance and speed of the resulting motion and these in turn became part of more complex compositions.

We were aware from the start that the images captured by a traditional camera were limited to a single viewpoint, fixing the photographic eye in time. Whether the picture is of a speeding bullet or a still life, the camera is limited by its position and temporal mechanics. Viewing all surfaces of a figure in a single instant places the viewer outside the frame of traditional lens-based perspectival vision, and with the photographic data produced by a 3-D scanner the views of the body become omni-directional. This allows an unlimited number of viewpoints to be derived from a single scan, and in visual terms the result is similar to surrounding the subject with an infinite number of eyes that can see all sides of an object at once. In further work we used this quality of the scanner to explore the camera's spatial relationship to the subject as well as the topology of the figure.

Our software now allows more complex interactions with the models and out-puts motion files. In the completed animations the body, shown from more than one viewpoint, can assemble and disassemble itself and at times dance across the screen in a macabre snowfall of thin slices.

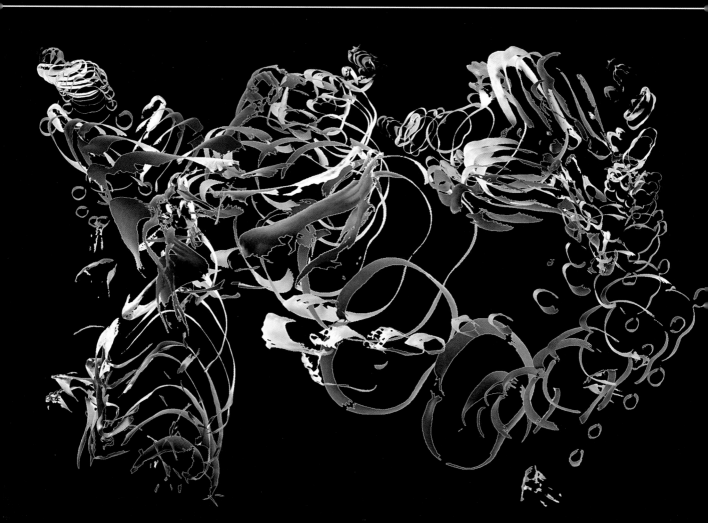

REFIGURING THE FIGURE

Imaging the Body in Contemporary Art and Digital Media

Alicia Imperiale

The mapping of live bodies is investigated here through the work of four contemporary visual artists: Mona Hatoum, Tim Hawkinson, Lilla LoCurto and Bill Outcault. How do artists transgress the opaque surface of the body to capture complex multidimensional spatial and temporal phenomena? Is the work printed on a flat surface, a deformed topological skin, or is it presented as time-based moving images? These questions probe the capacity of the flat surface to contain complex spatial and temporal phenomena and point to other representational modalities.[1]

A map is a construction that is simultaneously a translation of real phenomena and an abstraction of that translation. A map always exists in an uncanny relationship with the real as it is simultaneously an abstraction, a condition of opening up, of pointing towards new conditions, new spaces and new projects.

The game of traditional cartography has been how to represent complex multidimensional spatial and temporal information on a flat surface. In order to expand our idea of this surface and the complex relationships held on and across it, we may look to knots and topological geometry to understand the potential of a new range of complex models and spaces. For example, one could point to the development of isochrone maps, where mapping data is not simply presented in two dimensions but has the potential to deform space in relation to diverse synchronicities that exist in the data presented.

Velocity or speed can affect the perception of space. This difference in speed could be expressed in the deformation of an isochrone map that is less dependent on actual distance than on perceived distances. An isochrone map can enable spatial distances to be measured in time and allow for a fluid change of order and continuity.[2] This example is important as it points to the link between advanced analog representations and time-based digital modes of representation.

Advances in digital mapping techniques have changed and extended the limits of viewing and representing our bodies and the world. These new techniques allow for a verisimilitude and accuracy of information, and propose a new way of interacting with this information in the space of the computer. Information is no longer necessarily limited to projection onto a flat surface, since the information from a 3-D laser scan exists as a series of points in computer space. The viewer may move within this new map without a predetermined fixed point of view.

These digital techniques also permit artists to visualize the complexity of the

OPPOSITE:
Lilla LoCurto and Bill Outcault, self-portraits using cartography software from full-body laser scans, chromogenic print mounted on aluminum. Approximately 48 x 60 inches. SB#4-2. Courtesy of the artists and Frederieke Taylor Gallery, New York.

body in new ways and reveal the hidden depths and relations behind the surface of the body. Contemporary digital scanning techniques are used by artists not only to document a live body but to permit recombinant possibilities afforded by working within the projective space of the digital.

The human body is extraordinarily complex. It is an organism divided internally into differentiated and interpenetrating strata that slip from outside to inside in a continuous way.[3] The skin of the body is a surface of maximum interface and intensity, a space of flux, of oscillating energies. What does this mean for artists in terms of mapping? How may artists move past the surface of the body to explore the hidden depths of the body's interior?

Our bodies are, on the surface, so smooth, so simple.[4] However, this surface simplicity is betrayed by internal complexity (our hides hide our complexity). Lymphatic, renal, sanguine, digestive and neural systems are complex parallel labyrinths, layered one upon the other, separate yet coordinated. How do we visualize, imagine and map the spaces that make up our opacity, our corporeality? How do we distinguish boundaries and make separations?

This is an elusive endeavor. The body's smooth surface might hide blind passages that are understood in only the most visceral way, but its apertures and folds extend these interior spaces into the world.

In her video installation 'Corps étranger', artist Mona Hatoum brings another dimension to mapping the human body, touching on issues of privacy, territory and gender. A tiny endoscopic camera (a kind of foreign body) was inserted into Hatoum and the resulting video shows the journey (in full color) through the terrain of her body. The video was then projected onto a circular screen, horizontally placed at floor level within a cylindrically enclosed space, itself an interior body. What was once interior and invisible became external and spatial.

Tim Hawkinson begins with the surface of his body and through a number of cuts and grafts translates that surface into a new set of surfaces. In his 'Skin Spin' and 'Lingum' he casts his entire body in latex. He then translates the complex surface by cutting the latex cast into a series of strips (lines), which are used as a roller to create the striations of the final print with ink on paper. In 'Taper', a tapering self-portrait, the artist imagines a gridded surface thrown over his body and uses this grid as a way to measure distortion in the cartographic surface in relation to the tip of his finger as the point of origin. He explores the body as a potentially infinite series of recombinant forms.

Lilla LoCurto and Bill Outcault employ a full-body scanner to make self-portraits. The laser scanner is in fact a line that passes on and over the contours of the surface of their bodies and translates the information gained from this into digital data. The artists have worked with a team of mathematicians to develop complex cartography software that allows them to project this body data into a series of flat

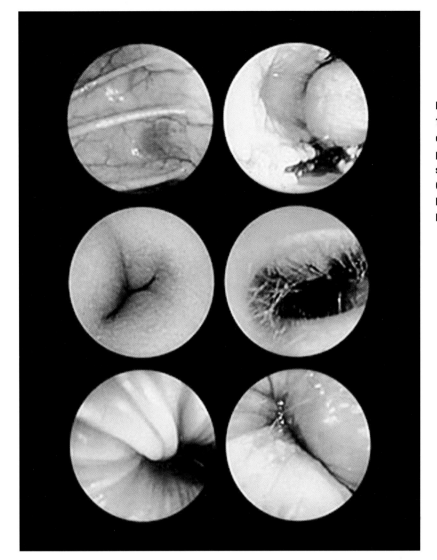

Mona Hatoum, '*Corps étranger*', 1994 video installation with cylindrical wooden structure, video projector, amplifier and four speakers (350 x 300 x 300 cm). Collection, Musée National d'Art Moderne, Centre Georges Pompidou, Paris.

projections. New digital tools have enabled them to create constantly changing maps that navigate the complexity of their bodies. In work resulting from the same data, LoCurto and Outcault have used the scans (separated into horizontal sections) to assemble and reassemble their bodies in a time-based 3-D animation (see 'Bodies Unfolding: self-portrait.map', pp 26–33).

A common theme for all the artists mentioned above is the elusiveness of the body. The seemingly simple task of mapping the body's dynamic form is complicated by our inability to determine where one surface ends and another begins. What we see most strikingly in the work of LoCurto and Outcault is the way new digital tools complicate the search for boundaries and edges. Here the skin of the body is translated into a flexible network of points that can be combined in infinite ways through movement and time. Beginning with the work of Mona Hatoum and ending with LoCurto and Outcault, we see artists working with the dynamic refiguration of bodily space.

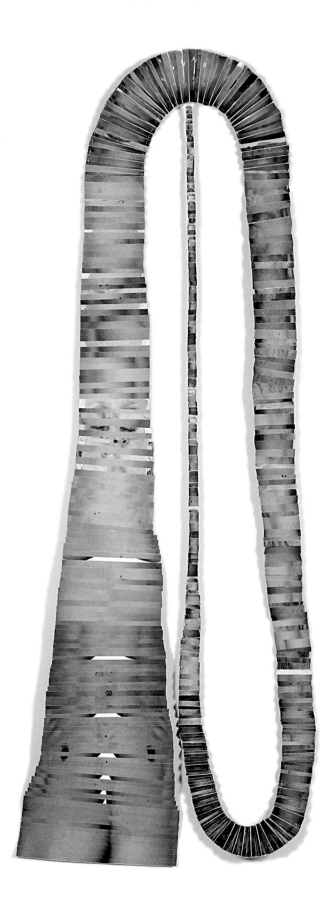

Tim Hawkinson, 'Taper', 1999.
Photo montage (48′ x 81¹⁄₂′).
Courtesy of Ace Gallery, Los
Angeles.

Gilles Deleuze proposed a definition of mapping that is useful for expanding our conception of the virtual and its relationship to cartography. We might think of a map as a registration of 'dynamic trajectories', which in turn open up and initiate other trajectories. The notion of dynamic trajectories and its parallel, maps of 'intensities', is how Deleuze explains the potential of cartography:

> Maps should not be understood only in extension, in relation to a space constituted by trajectories. There are also maps of intensity, of density, that are concerned with what fills space, what subtends the trajectory.[5]

This is a compelling idea that seems to be investigated intuitively in the movement from line to surface in the work of these artists.

Pierre Lévy provides us with another way of understanding virtuality and its relationship to mapping. Lévy focuses on the Latin root *virtualis* ('strength' or 'power') to emphasize that the virtual has potential rather than actual existence and that the virtual 'tends towards actualization without concretization'.[6] Lévy states that the virtual follows a line that ruptures classical ideas of space and time. Things can exist in parallel and 'distributive systems'.[7] If space and time are no longer coexistent, then the act of mapping may be liberated from these constraints. Synchronic events that occur in diverse (or non-existent) places can be related and mapped and may be shown as a network of relations. This is what we see in parametric design, or very simply in the translations made when a physical object is digitized and reconfigured.

The potential for infinite combinations is the virtual in mapping. We might consider mapping as a way to document real phenomena, but it is perhaps better to consider it more like writing a text that negotiates, travels and narrates without seeking a fixed conclusion.

To map is to work in continual flux – a map's reading is never fixed.

Notes

1 See the author's *New Flatness: Surface Tension in Digital Architecture*, Birkhauser-Verlag (Basel), 2000, and the essay 'Digital skins: Architecture of surface', in Ellen Lupton, *SKIN: Surface, Substance and Design*, Princeton Architectural Press (New York), 2002 for an expanded discussion of the digital and topological surfaces in contemporary design.

2 Bernard Cache, example adapted from 'A Plea for Euclid' (http://architettura.supereva.it/extended/19990501/index_en.htm).

3 The discussion of bodies arises from the Deleuzian discussion of the layering and folding of matter that forms all bodies, as discussed in the texts: Gilles Deleuze, *The Fold – Leibniz and the Baroque*, University of Minnesota Press (Minneapolis), 1993, and Bernard Cache, *Earth Moves: The Furnishing of Territories*, MIT Press (Cambridge, Mass), 1995.

4 Mark C Taylor, *Hiding*, University of Chicago Press (Chicago), 1997, p 18.

5 Gilles Deleuze, *Essays Clinical and Critical: 'What Children Say'*, University of Minnesota Press (Minneapolis), 1997, p 64.

6 Pierre Lévy, *Becoming Virtual: Reality in the Digital Age*, Plenum Press (New York), 1998, p 23.

7 Ibid, p 29.

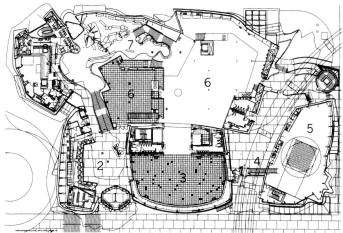

Aerial view and plan,
Experience Music Project, 2000.

MAPPING CURVES

An interview with James Glymph of Frank O Gehry and Associates

Mike Silver

MS: *In the last 20 years you have pioneered the use of computers in architecture. Your work at the office of Frank O Gehry and Associates has been hailed as ground-breaking. How did you get started and what is your background?*

JG: In the 1960s I started like everyone else who was interested in architecture, with a five-year professional degree program.

MS: *Did you study computing?*

JG: Only a little. Back in the days of mainframes, Fortran and punchcards computing didn't really have anything to do with architecture. And after school I pursued a pretty straightforward professional career as a designer who could work on technical problems in a professional office. I drew with ink on velum. What really interested me in those days was the relationship between the art of design and the science of building.

MS: *When did you start working with computers?*

JG: After a few years in Hawaii I moved to Seattle where I started to work with early software packages, though these were nothing more than automated drafting systems. This was in the 1970s. Later, in the 1980s when I went to work on the Santiago Convention Center with Arthur Eriksson and the engineering firm Horst Berger, I became involved with more interesting stuff. The engineers working on the LA Convention Center specialized in air-supported and tensegrity structures, and had developed a program for designing fabric structures (the project had a large tent-like roof that was designed and analyzed digitally). This was my first exposure to computing that attempted to simulate the physical behavior of real structures. At the time it was a rather laborious process to set up parametric models that could allow you to explore alternative design approaches in virtual space. But still this was the moment when I became interested in computing not as a way of automating the production of construction documents but as a technique for facilitating the design and fabrication processes.

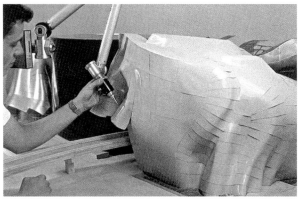

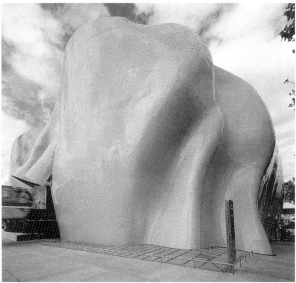

**Ferro arm collecting points on a physical
model, Experience Music Project, 2000.**

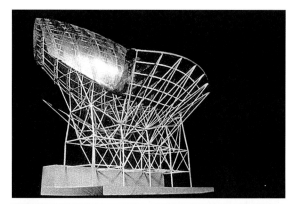

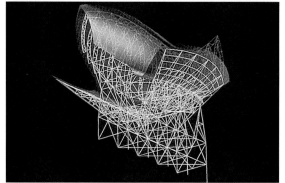

Barcelona Olympic Village, 1992.

MS: *When did you start to work for Frank Gehry?*

JG: Eventually I moved to Southern California where I met Frank through Jim Freed, who was working on the LA Convention Center. Frank had won the competition for the Disney Concert Hall and was looking for someone to give his office some in-house expertise on the process of building construction. This was a time when he wanted to go places in design that seemed feasible but often involved the difficult task of convincing clients, contractors and executive architects that daring work was possible. The Minneapolis Art Museum and American Center in Paris were already under construction. Many of us were using extremely cumbersome tech-niques for documenting the models that Frank and his staff were making by hand, using measuring probes, sticks, glass boxes and projectors to get two-dimensional drawings from 3-D forms. The process was creating a lot of problems. In1989 I met Bill Mitchell who was then at Harvard. He gave us a survey of what was happening in the world of advanced computer modeling. After this we started to search for software but there were no architectural programs at the time that would let us study complex surfaces, develop forms, manage data and analyze complex structures. So we expanded our search to include the stuff being used in the auto-motive and aerospace industries. This is where we found CATIA (computer-aided three-dimensional interactive applications).

MS: *When did the scanning and mapping tools come into the office? Can you describe what they were and how they worked?*

JG: We began to use what was called the Fire Fly system, a series of triangulated infrared cameras that would calculate the position of a wand used to take points from a physical 3-D model. It was funny because there were these skylights in the office, and if you took measurements in the morning these would differ from those taken in the afternoon. This was because temperature affects infrared light; we would get fragmented results where a surface recorded at one time of the day would not line up with another surface taken from the same form but recorded at a different time. This system was later replaced with a more accurate scanning device called a ferro arm. We also looked at point cloud generating devices but these did not work well with our process of design.

MS: *At the Yale Symposium on Digital Mapping you showed a series of images illustrating the simulation of panel deformations on a physical model that had been digitized. Can you describe the program and how it works?*

JG: The sculptural landmark Frank designed in Barcelona's Olympic Village (1992)

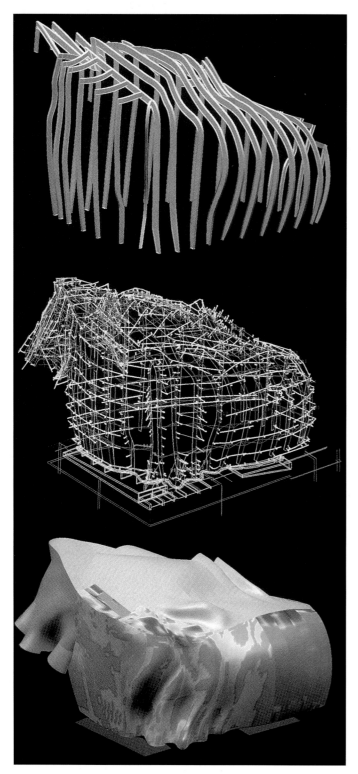

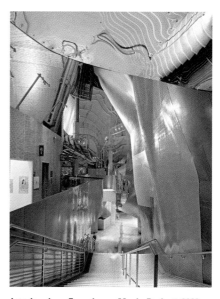

Interior view, Experience Music Project, 2000.

CATIA, steel structure and panel simulations,
Experience Music Project, 2000.

Interior view, steel structure, Experience Music
Project, 2000.

was the first project we worked on with CATIA. One of the problems was developing the skin for the structure. It was essentially a process of folding Venetian blinds around a fish. There were parts of the structure that we wanted to analyze to see how the woven stainless-steel skin would fold over the structure. In places the covering had to be taken through some pretty hard curves and we did not want to crease or deform the metal. We used the develop function in CATIA to determine which cladding techniques were best suited to the form. A similar process was used to design the panel system for the Experience Music Project (EMP) in Seattle. This is the project I showed at Yale.

MS: *How do you see the conception of architecture's physical constitution being transformed by these new simulation techniques? Will the computer provide the architect with a new way of understanding materials?*

JG: Frank works with physical models. He uses paper to represent sheet metal or maybe clay for a form that will be milled. We don't use the computer to replace any fundamental aspects of the practice of architecture, and certainly the understanding of a given material is something a designer must develop directly. Computer simulations today, and probably into the future, will never be able to reproduce the same open and creative understanding of materials because that understanding is invented. If you develop a sensibility around wood or metal and you decide how it should look or how it will be formed, then you can go back to the computer and tell it to simulate those behavioral qualities. Yet while CATIA has some pretty interesting analysis tools, none of them are pure – they are all fudged in some way. I don't think that design is rational the way programming is.

MS: *Was this analysis tool strictly a part of CATIA? Were you using off-the-shelf parts of the program or did you customize it in-house?*

JG: We have worked with Dauslt in helping to refine and develop CATIA. And we also have programmers in the office. Denis Sheldon, who has a background in both computing and architecture, was responsible for the EMP panel simulations. On the EMP project he used a Gaussian algorithm to analyze Frank's model so that we could determine which areas of its curved surface might be problematic. A color display lets you know how much you are distorting the material. The red and blue areas that show up on-screen tell you if the form is pushing the materials too far. Denis has also looked at Hollywood animation effects like those used to simulate flags blowing in the wind, and has developed algorithms that can be used in the office to simulate draping effects. But these are still a pretty rough approximation of real material behavior.

MS: *With the mapping system your office uses to convert hand-made forms into computer data there is a concerted effort to maintain the specificity of the original object, for example the maquette shaped by Gehry himself. With these newer simulation technologies the mapping of the initial form is augmented and refined. Do the changes in the overall shape produced by the simulation have an effect on the way Gehry works? Is there a kind of feedback happening in the process?*

JG: Frank is involved in every step of the process. Using ruled surfaces we tried to rebuild Frank's handmade models on the computer. These computer models were then printed in 3-D and compared to the original. The new version looked absolutely dead. It had no life – none of the energy of the original. And this was not just some esoteric observation made by a few people in the office – everyone noticed it.

MS: *What happened?*

JG: It was obvious. The compound curves of the original model reflected light in a way that the ruled surfaces did not. Although very subtle, they added a perceptible tension to the building's skin, like it was pumped up somehow. Everything got straightened out by the ruled lines used to approximate Frank's model.

MS: *From a computing and construction management standpoint, what part of the Mapping Symposium interested you the most?*

JG: I was surprised because the symposium was not just a gathering of architects, contractors and academics. The different disciplines present at Yale really made the importance of fluid information exchange very clear. How do you deal efficiently with large sets of data? I particularly liked the 9/11 GIS presentation made by John Ziegler. It highlighted the ability of the computer to rapidly assemble vast quantities of highly accurate information at a moment of crisis. We really need to reform the way various trades in the construction and design industry use, organize and share data. Many of our management procedures are inefficient. We need to wipe the slate clean and reformulate the process so that everyone works together in a more fluid way. This seems possible only when people are faced with a crisis. At the World Trade Center site there was no choice – everyone had to pull together and recreate order from the ground up. This needed to happen fast and efficiently. Why can't we do the same thing for architecture?

MAPPING TIME

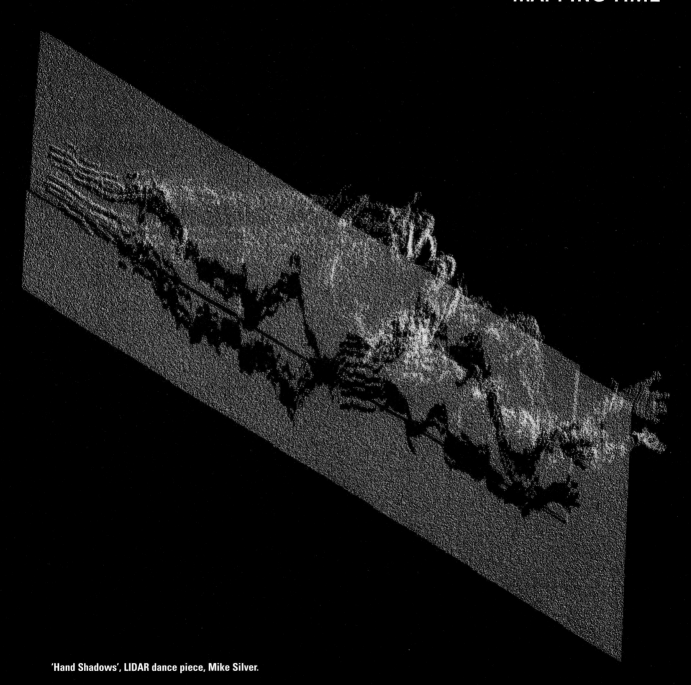

'Hand Shadows', LIDAR dance piece, Mike Silver.

NETWORKING MAPS

GIS, Virtualized Reality and The World Wide Web

Mike Silver and Diana Balmori

'We are not cartographers … we are spatial data managers.'
Joel Morrison, Director of the Ohio State Center for Mapping[1]

'The average American is caught on camera eight to 10 times a day.'
Associated Press[2]

Cartography, a term derived from the word for chart (*charte*) or drawing, has in recent years undergone a radical transformation. Like many other disciplines, the practice of mapping now incorporates a wide variety of information technologies and surveillance tools. The widespread accessibility of the Internet, the rapid proliferation of new data-acquisition devices and fast computers have redefined the map-maker's art in terms very different from those rooted in the history of paper.

Through the work of John Ziegler, Konrad Perlman, Brian McGrath and Takeo Kanade, this essay explores four aspects of spatial data management: surveillance, collation, interactivity and simulation.

John Ziegler of Spacetrack Inc used geographic information systems (GIS) software to coordinate data owned or produced by groups, government agencies and private companies working on the site of the World Trade Center collapse. As part of geographic information systems mapping operations (GISMOO), he helped produce coherent maps taken from surveys of a rapidly changing context. As the ultimate collating technology, GIS also served as a way to combine different types of information about Ground Zero into a single database of layered files. Ziegler writes:

> We couldn't possibly have redrawn maps of the 9/11 site at the speed they were needed. Time was essential. Every ten minutes you had a changed situation. Information from light direction and ranging (LIDAR) scanners, mapping satellites and photogrammetry surveys all had to be drawn-up and integrated. As the situation kept changing we could track what was unfolding day by day. Very important too was that these maps could be attached to other kinds of data – how many people were in the area, where the hazard zones were located, etc.[3]

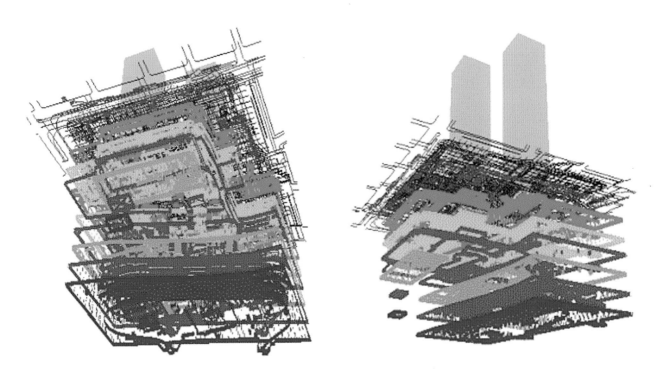

**GIS maps of the World Trade Center,
John Ziegler, Space Track Inc.**

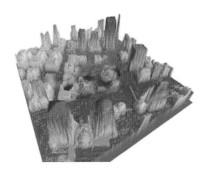  

LIDAR scans of the World Trade Center.

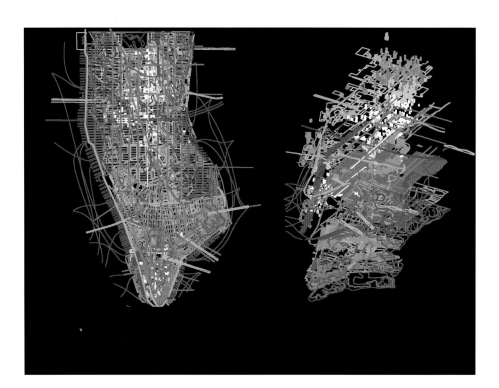

'Manhattan Timeformations',
Brian McGrath and Mark
Watkins.

Brian McGrath's 'Manhattan Timeformations' (www.skyscraper.org/timeformations),
not unlike the layered system of Ziegler's 9/11 GIS, extends the paradigm of networked maps to an extreme, displaying the story of New York City over many years
in a 3-D space located on the World Wide Web. While GIS databases tend to be
restricted to a network of local users, McGrath's website is globally accessible:

> Techniques of layering, seriality and transparency were complemented by the
> destabilizing power of interactivity, movement and animation, effects result-
> ing from the modeling tools we used to map the history of office building
> speculation on Manhattan Island … The website is both a time-line of office
> building construction and a layering of historical maps, hybridizing two-dimen-
> sional graphic devices into a four-dimensional diagram.[4]

Extending this four-dimensionality even further, Takeo Kanade (a robotics engineer
at Carnegie Mellon University) has designed the 'Virtualized Reality' machine – a
distributed network of tiny cameras the outputs of which are recalibrated by computers to form a real-time 3-D image of physical space. These networked cameras
can monitor events as they happen from any angle or vantage point. Users can tran-
scend the frontality of the traditional video or movie screen and navigate the world
from any vantage point.

This system, originally designed as a new way to view sports events, destabi-
lizes the hegemonic centrality endemic to the disciplinary regimes studied by

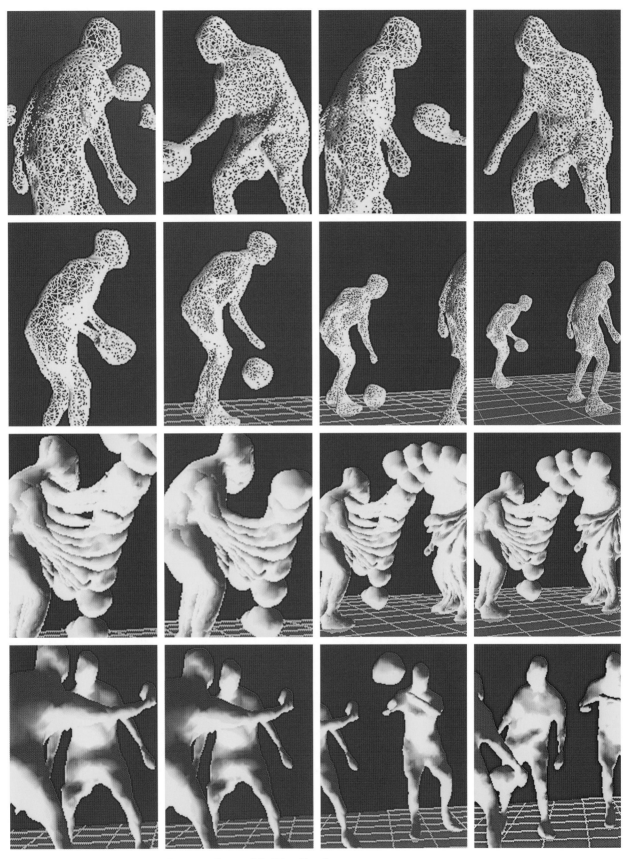

Real-time 3-D captures of a basketball game: surface models, Takeo Kanade.

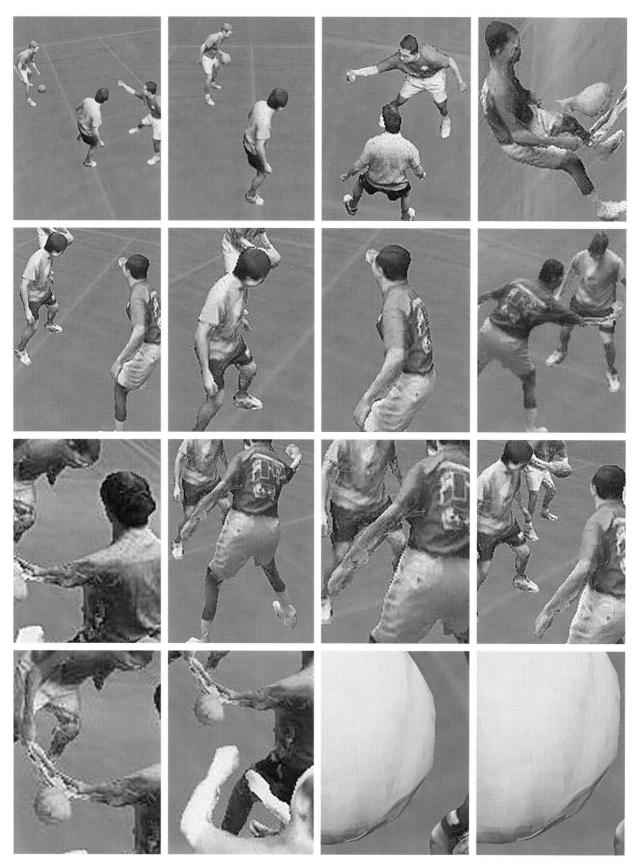

Real-time 3-D captures of a basketball game: texture-mapped bodies, Takeo Kanade.

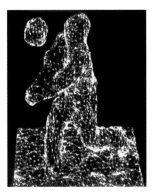

Live scene to 'Virtualized Reality', Takeo Kanade.

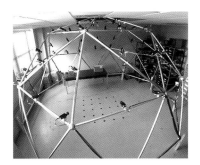

'Virtualized Reality' stage, Takeo Kanade.

Texture mapped scene, Takeo Kanade.

Foucault in his famous work on Jeremy Bentham. The centralized plan of the panopticon is replaced by a network of stations evenly distributed in space. Kanade's 'Virtualized Reality' machine permits a surveillance level unprecedented in the history of architecture. Both the virtualized spectator and those being watched overlap like ghosts haunting an alternate universe. Drifting like specters these eyes and bodies (invisible to each other) coexist in a common space without ever touching. Disembodied by electronic tools, the panoptic centrality key to understanding Foucault's 'carceral' space disappears. The single perspectival view (crows nest, observation tower, command post) is replaced by multifarious eyes that exist everywhere and nowhere simultaneously. Space becomes super-saturated by vision.

While Ziegler, McGrath and Kanade organize the flow of spatial information in their own way, if taken together each adds up to a system that would be more than

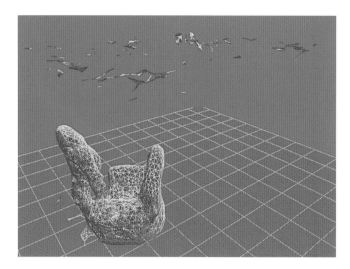

**Real-time 3-D mesh model,
Takeo Kanade.**

the sum of its parts. Not yet in existence, this system (a 3-D, real-time, networked map accessible on the World Wide Web) is, according to Joel Morrison, a very real possibility – one that constitutes the ultimate dream of the map-maker. Such a map would operate on-line, receiving updated information in real time from a network of distributed sensors that constantly monitor space. Hyperlinked to this mapping interface are any number of sites containing logistical, demographic or economic information relevant to the site being observed.

This 'spectropticon', assembled from the root words for 'ghost' (specter) and 'vision' (optics), is meant to challenge the centralized paradigm of surveillance defined by panoptic architectures on the one hand while destabilizing the order of tyrannically managed networks on the other. The absolute divorce of data space from physical space is augmented in this model by a mirror universe modified by actions mapped in the world while simultaneously detached from them through the agency of electronic networks. On the Internet, issues of surveillance are complicated and I use the model of the 'spectropticon' here as a way to hybridize the idea of spaces that are electronically decentered yet physically place-bound.

If this map is left open for access by anyone then it becomes a public space that exists both in-situ through surveillance and distributed everywhere as an interactive system. But if the spectropticon becomes the property of a few, a 'false web', then it can be turned, as Foucault has warned us, into an instrument for the exercise of a power, one 'that seeks ideally to reach the most elementary particle – a faceless gaze that (transforms) the whole social body into a field of perception: thousands of eyes posted everywhere, mobile attentions ever on alert, a long hierarchized network'.[5] In this schema the pathways of information exchange are tightly controlled by a central agent or political body so that the possible formation of a true network, one that is intentionally left open, is precluded by the inscrutable operations of a single authority.

It is important to note that complexity in the spectropticon can emerge in only a milieu of freely interconnected users. The idea of the network itself becomes the

**3-D interactive GIS model,
Konrad Perlman.**

infrastructure for a reality that extends well beyond the reach of a single author. The network encourages interaction, thus preparing the way for emergent phenomena and the complex interactions of a variety of forces, entities and subjects. If indeed this map is ever produced, perhaps we will see it as something more than just a surveyor's tool. Rather we might understand it as a parallel universe intimately connected to the vicissitudes and flux of our physical environment.

Of course the benefits of such a map would be enormous. The adaptability and scope of its networked spaces could easily incorporate many of the features currently designed into the most advanced GIS platforms. As Konrad Perlman writes:

> For each alternative scenario that is drawn into a GIS scene, impact models can be generated to show the additional residents, employees, cars, etc that are generated by a proposed development … GIS completes the integration of planning, architecture, zoning and urban design. Consequently an infinite number of studies can be developed if the data is available.[6]

This interactive space, once connected to the Web, would become the ultimate design simulator functioning both as a system that continuously monitors the city and as a public forum facilitating the experimental exchange of ideas. Here development strategies for the built environment (urban, rural, suburban) could be tested in ways that permit an unprecedented level of public involvement and flexible democratic exchange.

Notes
1 Quoted from an (unpublished) conversation at the Ohio State Center for Mapping.
2 Associated Press, 'Sniper's face still a blank', *New Haven Register*, 17 October 2002.
3 Cited from an (unpublished) interview with Diana Balmori, June 2002.
4 Brian McGrath and Mark Watkins, 'Urban mapping and the Web', unpublished.
5 Michel Foucault, *Discipline and Punish: the Birth of The Prison*, Vintage Books (New York), 1977, p 214.
6 Konrad Perlman, 'Interactive 3-D GIS: Changing perspectives in time and space for architects, city planners, and the community', unpublished.

THE POWER OF THE IMAGE TO PROMOTE SCIENCE

Eric Heller

One has only to look at the tremendous popular and professional impact of astrophotography to understand the importance of images in science and science communication. Scientific disciplines with good pictures are rich in resources that keep them well funded and moving forward. Fields such as astronomy are exporters of their imagery, enriching other fields such as atomic physics. Outreach is increasingly important at a time when the support of scientific endeavors is waning. Some fields, such as paleontology, manufacture their imagery; for example the reconstruction of fossil remains for public viewing, or through imaginative illustrations of immense creatures from the past. And Hollywood's use of stunning computer-generated graphics has likewise had a profound impact on the public's understanding of new ideas and discoveries.

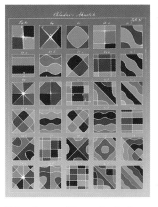

Taken from an illustration by E Chladni, showing nodal patterns of a square metal plate (nodes are in black).

Sciences that target objects large enough to photograph with an optical microscope or larger must skillfully exploit the tools of visual communication. Even chemistry with its focus on structures and processes about a thousand times too small to capture with a camera has a standard iconography with which to communicate its results to the public. In the same way, nanotechnology has garnered wide support for its endeavors using visual descriptions of novel geometric structures such as nanotubes and quantum dots.

Through the work of Chladni, Ørsted and the Weber brothers, this essay will explore the link between good images and good science, and will briefly describe my own attempts to explain quantum mechanics, using a rich lexicon of graphic maps and rendered images.

Chladni and Ørsted

Ernst Chladni (1756–1827) was a major figure in Napoleon's day. Not only did Chladni invent and popularize the visualization of wave patterns, he also was the first to realize that meteors came from space. In 1787 he published the results of his experiments with vibrating metal disks. In 'Entdeckungen über die Theorie des Klanges' (Discoveries Concerning the Theory of Sound, 1787) he mapped out the complex interaction of soundwaves produced on disks covered with small resin particles. When stroked with a violin bow the resin would move to areas on the disk that were not vibrating. These regions, called nodes, formed unique graphic patterns. Chladni, well-known for his lectures combining sound and vision, was

OPPOSITE:
'Transport IX' electron flows in two dimensions. Electrons injected downward make patterns known as 'cusps' and then branches as they negotiate a bumpy landscape.

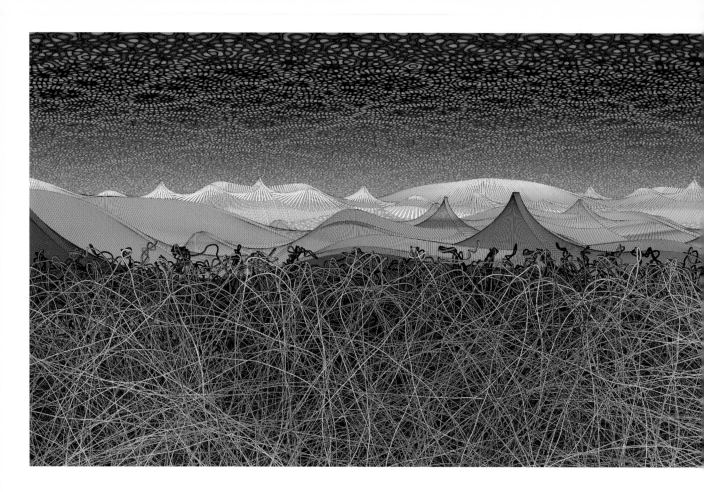

'Chaos Universe': an image showing three kinds of chaos: waves (top), stroboscopic images of chaotic rotating hinged bars (middle), and electron paths in a wire (bottom).

perhaps the first scientist to develop multimedia techniques for presenting new ideas. (He was also famous for inventing the euphonium, a musical instrument that produced pure tones when rubbed with a moist finger.)

A strong supporter of science, Napoleon described Chladni's work as 'sound made visible', and during one demonstration he also suggested that patterns produced on irregularly shaped plates would be much harder to describe. This observation, also made by Chladni, can be taken as a first step in the study of quantum chaos. Because chaotic patterns are intrinsically complex they remain (and to some extent will always remain) unexplained.

Chladni and his images also strongly influenced Hans Christian Ørsted (1777–1851), who discovered electromagnetism. Although he later distanced himself from the non-rigorous Schelling-inspired *Naturphilosophen*, Ørsted was not quite a modern scientist in that he saw little distinction between empiricism and metaphysics. To this day his writings still inspire pseudoscientific speculation. Ørsted had a strong attachment to the patterns and physics behind wave phenomena. In his time he improved Chladni's techniques and wrote extensively about new discoveries.

Chladni patterns are still a subject of contemporary research; everything from violin acoustics to automobile vibrations is investigated with more sophisticated

tools based on his original idea. It is safe to say that Chladni's sound-and-vision experiments had, and still have, an enormous impact on the development of scientific communication techniques. If Chladni had described his work with only words, the results of his analysis may not have had as profound an impact on the public imagination as it did.

BELOW:
Illustration showing the wave pattern that results when liquid mercury is dropped on a Petri dish containing more mercury, Ernst Heinrich Weber and Wilhelm Eduard Weber, 1825.

The Weber brothers

The German scientists Wilhelm Eduard Weber (1804–91) and Ernst Heinrich Weber (1795–1878) investigated wave patterns traveling through various media. In 1825 they wrote *Wellenlehre* (Wave Studies), a book containing two remarkable graphic representations of waves moving in a pool of mercury.[1] One of these meticulous drawings, which consists of around 500,000 handmade stipples, was cited by Harry Robin in his book *The Scientific Image: From Cave to Computer*.[2] The Webers considered themselves followers of Chladni.

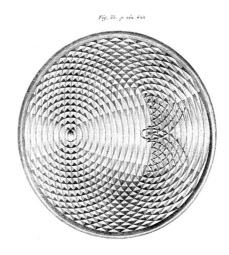

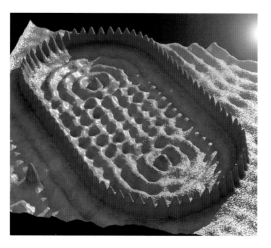

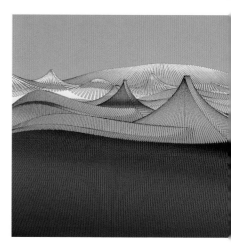

ABOVE LEFT:
Scanning tunneling microscope image of a quantum corral, made of 76 iron atoms sitting on the surface of copper.

ABOVE CENTRE:
'Exponential', formed from 2-D electron flow.

Visualizing quantum mechanics and quantum chaos

The quantum world is intrinsically invisible. The public has a difficult time imagining its structures and laws. In Martin Kemp's *Visualizations: the Nature of Art and Science*, a book containing more than 70 images, only one section on Feynman diagrams comes anywhere close to explaining the wave nature of matter.[3] How can one visually communicate the intrinsically invisible? Quantum mechanics (and its unruly cousin, quantum chaos) are the elements out of which all visual systems are built, but they are too small to be imaged directly. Depicting the atomic and nanoscale domain is therefore subject to interpretation – there are no 'correct' pictures awaiting discovery. The scanning tunneling microscope (STM) experiments of IBM's Almaden Eigler group (see above left) are tastefully rendered images taken from data that represent invisible quantum waves. At the same time they are simply direct height maps of current flow versus position. An untrained viewer might mistake these images for photographs – pictures that are more real than they actually are – though there may be little harm in this.

An image like 'Exponential' is a fairly literal rendition of numerically simulated flows in a two-dimensional electron gas. Such gases are produced on the micron scale as a result of semiconductor fabrication. However, the doping Si atoms that donate electrons to the gas are close neighbors and the resulting opposite charged attractions make potential hills and dales in the energy landscape. Electrons in the sample are forced to negotiate these irregularities causing a perfectly uniform flow of electrons to branch off in complex ways.

The methods used to produce these images vary. Some, like the 'Transport' series, are drawn by code written in Fortran which writes data to a very large raw byte array, ready for reading into image-editing software. Here, hue and contrast, transparency and gradient values are adjusted to give the image its final appearance. Other images go through a succession of mesh surface rendering, alteration and transparency in Illustrator, rasterization and the steps above in Photoshop. Various algorithms are used to intensify colors and recode the data within the Fortran, and these give a remarkable range of effects.

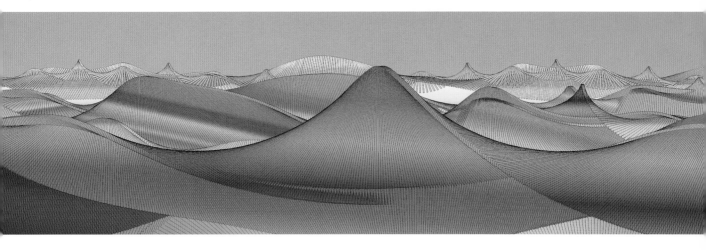

Visual discoveries

Computer renderings of data provide another way of seeing. In the past there was a strong aversion to presenting pictures as scientific evidence, and this has of course thwarted the comprehension of basic ideas by making the language of science increasingly obscure and specialized. Consider the case of Laplace, who rejected the use of diagrams in his writings. Laplace felt that explanatory graphics were unnecessary crutches. Mary Somerville, who translated Laplace's *Mécanique Céleste*, shared this view, suggesting: 'Diagrams are not employed in Laplace's work because they are not necessary for those versed in analysis'.[4] However, the graphics and animations commonplace in today's PowerPoint presentations are a radical departure from the way scientific ideas were previously communicated, and restrictions and rules established by figures such as Laplace have slowly begun to erode.

Rotating rotators: stroboscopic images of chaotic rotating hinged bars.

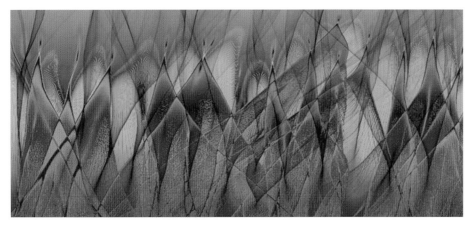

'Transport VII': electron paths make cusps as they are focused by hills and dales in the material they travel through.

'Transport II': electrons injected at the center in all directions make cusps and then branches as they negotiate a bumpy landscape. The darker areas indicate where more electrons have traveled.

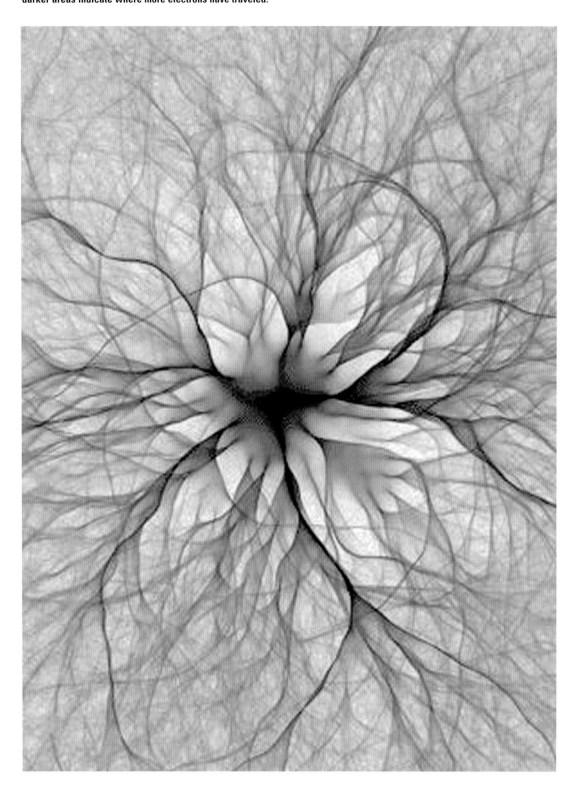

The structures clearly visible in images like 'Transport II' were not previously known, but making images of large regions later revealed new information. In fact, it would have been possible years earlier to simply plot this phenomenon, but the prejudice against images precluded such work. Not all graphical methods are equal in their ability to reveal information, and certain scarring phenomena were probably missed by MacDonald and Kauffman in their first attempt to investigate numerically determined eigenstates in chaotic systems (specifically the stadium billiard). MacDonald, in his 1979 Berkeley PhD thesis, plotted the nodal structure of the eigenstates (à la Chladni!) and added some cruder 'waterfall' plots of probable wave-function densities. Although in a few cases MacDonald noticed the correspondence of 'ridges running along their periodic orbits' (the hallmark of what we now call scarring), these were prematurely dismissed as anomalies. Had better graphics been available at the time, he would no doubt have been compelled to find a theoretical basis for the scars, which finally appeared in 1984.[5]

ABOVE LEFT:
'Caustic I': three-dimensional flow through random media is like light passing through a wavy surface of water. The light can be intercepted on a pool bottom. 'Caustic I' is a simulation of the light after it has passed through two successive pool surfaces onto a pool bottom – something hard to achieve in reality.

ABOVE RIGHT:
'Caustic II': this is similar to 'Caustic I', but after passing through seven surfaces.

Conclusion

There is no question that a long succession of scientists have done themselves and the public a favor by keenly exploiting our sense of sight. Until recently, however, such scientists were rare, mostly due to the prejudice against the use of figures and images in scientific writing. However, the changing attitudes to imagery within the scientific community, the accessibility of comprehensible modes of representation and the emergence of new technologies dedicated to the facile production of stunning graphics all point to a new golden age of scientific illustration.

Notes
1 Ernst Heinrich Weber and Wilhelm Eduard Weber, *Wellenlehre*, Leipzig, 1825.
2 Harry Robin, *The Scientific Image: From Cave to Computer*, HN Abrahams, 1992.
3 Martin Kemp, *Visualizations: the Nature of Art and Science*, University of California Press, 2001.
4 Mary Fairfax Greig Somerville, *Mechanism of the Heavens*, 1831.
5 EJ Heller, 'Bound state Eigenfunctions of classical chaotic systems: scars of periodic orbits', *Phys Rev Lett*, 53, 1515–18 (1984).

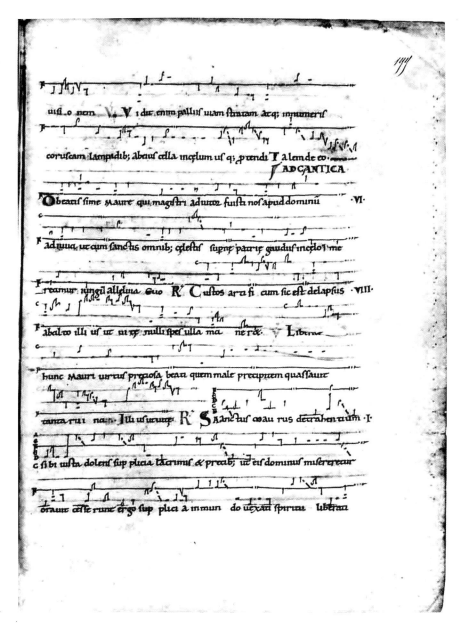

Example 1 **Page from eleventh-century manuscript from the Saint-Maur-des-Fossés monastery near Paris.**

Example 2 **Opening measures of Muzio Clementi's Sonatina in G Major, Op. 36 No. 2, 1797.**

MAPPING MUSICAL SPACE

Evan Jones

Musical notation exists in many forms and receives a diversity of realization. Some musical traditions are perpetuated in the absence of any notational method; some notational methods may be more or less specific about the pitch, rhythm, speed or loudness of the intended result; and some aspects of notated music (such as details of tone color) are usually left unwritten. When some form of notation is used, however, a unifying 'cartographic strategy' can most often be identified – that of plotting of frequency in the vertical dimension against time in the horizontal.

Examples 1–3, taken from three widely different periods of musical composition, provide a cross-section of different illustrations of the 'pitch versus time' strategy. To some (especially those familiar with traditional musical notation) this may seem to be an absolute requirement for comprehensibility. How else, one might ask, should we notate an ascending melody but with a line that ascends on the page from left to right? Indeed, this principle is quite pervasive, although there are certainly exceptions. The score to an ensemble work usually orders the parts from top to bottom in approximate pitch order, but the trajectories of the individual voices will result in frequent violations of this order.[1] Further, when the notes on a single staff are modified by accidentals, their vertical position may disagree with their pitch order. Nor is the correspondence between temporal order and horizontal notational order inviolable: the performer(s) may be invited or instructed to repeat, interpolate or omit certain notated sections of music, for example.[2] But as a general rule these correspondences hold.

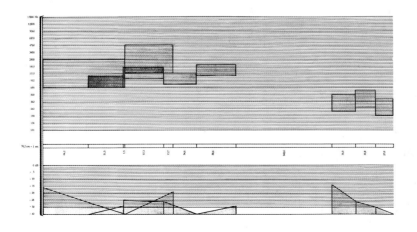

Example 3 **The first page of Karlheinz Stockhausen's electronic composition 'Studie II' (1954), representing 6.8 seconds of music. Pitch indicated by shapes in the upper section of the score; amplitude indicated by shapes in the lower section.**

It will be of interest, however, to consider some alternative modes of musical 'cartography' that do not follow this rule. These alternative cartographies interpret rather than notate the music. Musical materials are reconceived, their interrelationships revealed, and the trajectories between musical events traced within some field of musical potential. Various cartographies have arisen in the context of relatively recent scholarly explorations in music theory and analysis. While music theory seeks a general understanding of musical structure, music analysis examines particular pieces of music in the light of received theory. The two are, of course, inextricably related; every analytical project derives from some theoretical basis, and every theoretical pronouncement suggests an analytical application. Models of musical structure usually aim to capture aspects of one's experience of the music (perhaps the experience of someone very familiar with it) that the score may not reveal very clearly, and to display these aspects in some written form.

It seems to me that we can distinguish many of the current theoretical models from 'mere' notation – that is, written representations of music that are in some sense uninterpreted – by examining the way in which musical events are plotted on the page. Many representations of musical structure establish some sort of space, the navigation of which results in a realization of musical potential. The one-dimensional 'space' of the piano keyboard offers many possible options for traversing its expanse; the centuries' worth of music written for the piano comprise a certain fraction of the available options in this regard. But theoretical models often posit new kinds of adjacencies or modes of succession, other than adjacency or succession in pitch and/or time. While some of the spaces that we will examine here are strictly two-dimensional, others expand into a third dimension. In both cases new modes of musical 'measurement' translate inevitably into new modes of listening to and appreciating music.

Two-dimensional representations of musical structure

Most musicians are familiar with the 'circle of fifths', the closed succession of keys based on tonal centers related by perfect fifths. The interval of a fifth represents a very close relation in tonal music: two keys a fifth apart will share six out of seven notes in common.[3] Due to this closeness, the progression of key areas throughout a piece of music can be experienced as a journey around this circle of fifths.

Such a journey is traced in Example 4 (Figure 2 from Carpenter 1983). Each of the 14 numbered arrows corresponds to one of the many changes of key throughout the first movement of Beethoven's Piano Sonata Op. 57 (the *Appassionata*). Uppercase letters are used to represent major keys, while lowercase letters represent minor keys; these are arranged in two concentric circles of fifths so as to juxtapose relative major and minor keys at the same position on their respective circles. (Two keys which share all seven notes if no accidentals are used – for example

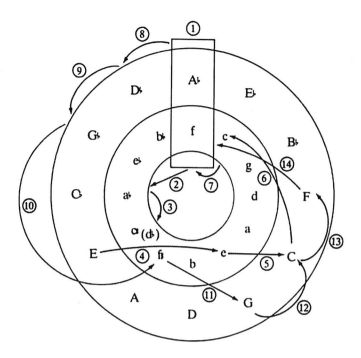

Example 4 **The tonal plan of the first movement of Beethoven's piano sonata Op. 57 (the *Appassionata*) as mapped by Carpenter, 1983.**

F minor and Ab major, which appear in the box at the top of this example – are defined as relatives.) Beethoven begins and ends in F minor, cycling twice completely around this double circle of fifths in a counterclockwise direction.[4]

Example 4 represents not only a tonal odyssey of startling scope and directional consistency but also, paradoxically, a certain openness of form. If perfectly pure fifths (sounding as a frequency ratio of 3:2) were deployed in such a manner, one would never regain exactly the same original key. Rather, for every complete cycle the pitch would change by an interval known as the Pythagorean comma (0.2346 of a semitone). It is only because the fifths on any keyboard instrument have been 'tempered', or reduced slightly in size from the 3:2 ideal, that closure is achieved in the manner suggested by the diagram.[5] Listeners accustomed to associating repeated motion by fifths with migration or departure may well experience the equivalent of a double-take as F minor is reapproached from the right side of the circle, having originally departed to the left.

Another two-dimensional reconfiguration of musical motion is shown in Example 5 (Figure 16 from Cohn 1997). The three trajectories plotted in Example 5 are representative of the musical excerpts given in Examples 6–8, composed by Brahms, Beethoven and Schubert, respectively. The space in which these trajectories are traced is a Tonnetz, best known from the eighteenth- and nineteenth-century writings of Leonhard Euler, Gottfried Weber, Arthur von Oettingen and (most notably) Hugo Riemann.[6] The nodes on this Tonnetz are occupied by the numbers 0 to 11, representing the 12 different notes in an octave (0 represents the note C in any octave, 1 represents any C#, and so on up to 11, which represents any B). These are arranged in a grid in a repeating pattern: the rows feature intervals of three semitones and the columns feature intervals of four semitones.[7]

Due to this intervallic patterning, all of the triangular formations shown on the

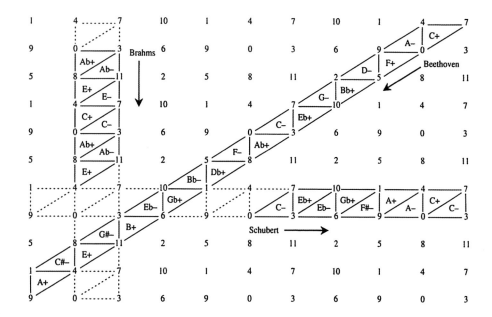

Example 5 **Opposing trajectories on the Tonnetz of the three musical excerpts given in Examples 6–8 (from Cohn 1997).**

Example 6 **Brahms, Concerto for Violin and Cello, Op. 102, Mvt 1, measures 270278 (from Cohn 1997).**

Example 7 **Beethoven, Symphony No. 9, Mvt 2, measures 143–176 (from Cohn 1991).**

Example 8 **Schubert, Overture to Die Zauberharfe, opening Andante (from Cohn 1997).**

Tonnetz connect three pitch classes to form a major or minor triad. The Beethoven excerpt in Example 7, for example, begins with a C-major triad followed by an A-minor triad; these are written as C+ and A− (respectively) in the upper right-hand corner of Example 5. Since each of these excerpts features a repeating harmonic pattern – known as a sequence – they each appear on the Tonnetz as following a straight path. The direction of each path is determined by the particular progressions found between triads in each of the excerpts. Of course, these directions are in no sense absolute: Brahms's passage is not of inherently 'downwards' character, even though it runs in a downwards direction on the page. The Tonnetz would be just as meaningful upside-down or under some rotation. But the opposition of these three trajectories (each running parallel to one of the three sides of any triadic triangle) is crucial, and would be retained under any alternate transformation of the space. This 'map' captures something of the identity and the incommensurability of these harmonic progressions, and speaks to the sense of momentum that characterizes any sequence.

Both kinds of 'cartography' that have so far been introduced are communicative of musical motion. In these and other cases, two-dimensional displacement is a metaphor for certain kinds of transformation or evolution in a piece of music. But musical experience can certainly exceed the bounds of two-dimensional Euclidean space; in live performance situations, arguably, it always does. When seeking to reconfigure the elements of a musical work so as to highlight some kind of metaphorical motion or development, two dimensions can sometimes seem rather limiting. For example, one might wish for a musical score in which the two axes of pitch and time are joined by a third axis representing loudness: imagine a stereoscopic score in which louder notes appeared closer and softer ones further away.

Relations of similarity or derivation are also important: a number of related motives or themes, given in traditional pitch-versus-time notation, could be juxtaposed in a third dimension representing the evolutionary compositional chain tying them together. The third dimension might even be time itself: an out-of-time diagram such as Carpenter's circle of fifths (Example 4) could be expanded into a cylinder – the length of which would measure the duration of the piece – and the circulating path she traces could be represented as a helix winding from one end to the other. Such 3-D representations would not only make a diagram such as Example 4 easier to read but would approach a more complete rendering of the multifaceted, non-Euclidean nature of musical experience.

Extending earlier Euclidean models into three dimensions

Some 3-D models of musical space already exist. A simple but highly significant perturbation of the pitch axis is proposed by Shepard (1964). Shepard tests the apparent proximity of complex tones consisting of stacked octaves. Since these

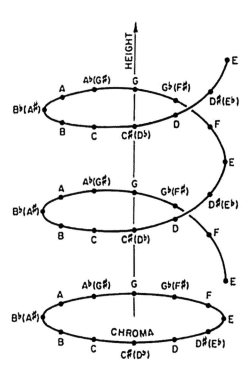

Example 9 **Shepard pitch helix (from Krumhansl 1990).**

tones have, in effect, no registral aspect, their succession in scalar order gives a paradoxical aural impression similar to that of the spiral pattern on a barbershop pole: a continuous ascent or descent will eventually lead back to the original tone. This effect is rendered in three dimensions in Example 9. The note names along the circle at the bottom of the example (labeled 'chroma') represent the complex tones containing each given note in every octave, and are thus equivalent to the numerical note designations in Example 5.[8] The helix ascends from this circle according to the frequency of particular tones, and returns to an imaginary pillar above each of the chroma every time the same note name is encountered (once every octave).

The distinction between single notes and so-called 'Shepard tones' is crucial to many aspects of music theory: sometimes the particular octave in which a pitch sounds is very much of interest and sometimes (particularly in studies of atonal music) that information is discarded. Shepard's experimental results – as embodied in this diagram – capture that distinction in a way that is easy to apprehend visually.

The Tonnetz, as well, has been subjected to various 3-D 're-imaginings'. The space diagrammed in Example 5 itself suggests the 3-D shape of a torus.[9] Note that the numerical elements in Example 5 repeat themselves both vertically and horizontally – every three elements vertically, every four elements horizontally. Therefore, any 3-by-4 subsection of this diagram is representative of the whole. The entire table, then, can be thought of in terms of any such subsection, doubly joined to itself: the top and bottom join together to form a cylinder, then the left and right sides of this cylinder join together to form a torus. The excerpts by Brahms, Beethoven and Schubert will follow their individual paths (always, as before, in fundamental opposition to each other) around the exterior of this toroidal shape.

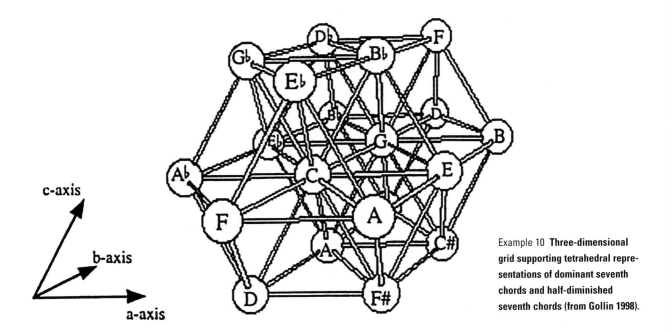

Example 10 **Three-dimensional grid supporting tetrahedral representations of dominant seventh chords and half-diminished seventh chords (from Gollin 1998).**

In contrast to the flat representation of the Tonnetz in Example 5, a toroidal representation captures the closed nature of the musical space it describes: notwithstanding the impression of motion or migration that these sequences convey, they will eventually return to their point of origin.

The Tonnetz has been extended into three dimensions by Vogel (1993), Lindley and Turner-Smith (1993), and Gollin (1998). In Example 10 (Gollin's Figure 2), a third axis joins the original two: while the a-axis and b-axis are defined by intervals of major thirds and perfect fifths, respectively, the c-axis features major seconds. Dominant seventh chords and half-diminished seventh chords obtain between the vertices of regular tetrahedrons throughout this structure. (One such tetrahedron, formed by vertices containing notes F, A, C and Eb, appears to be closest to the observer in the example.) This 3-D Tonnetz houses many harmonic progressions typical of the late-Romantic period, in which the pure triads of Example 5 are often avoided. Gollin describes a family of ten distinct operations within this Tonnetz to transform one seventh chord into another, referring to them as 'edge-flips' or 'vertex-flips' of the tetrahedrons involved. The choreography that emerges from Gollin's various flips itself conveys quite a musical impression.

The concept of a musical 'space' suggests potential rather than actual music; indeed, the spaces that we have so far encountered present neutral (perhaps sterile) geometries, which can be experienced on an emotional level only when they are inscribed by a composer's inspiration. Given this dependence, what do these models provide for us that we find worthwhile? I believe the importance of these and other music-theoretic models rests in their portrayal of certain non-contiguous musical events as spatially adjacent; this adjacency helps us to compare and connect the events to each other in a way not necessarily suggested by the standard pitch-versus-time notation.

Just as an interpreter (whether an analyst or a performer) posits relationships between the components of a piece of music beyond those communicated by the score, so too must a written expression of such an interpretation highlight musical relationships other than those shown as adjacencies of some kind in the score. Thus, both the circle of fifths and the Tonnetz disregard closeness in frequency altogether (as indicated by vertical displacement in a traditional score) in favor of new modes of harmonic closeness – measured on a circle of fifths by the number of fifths between keys, and on the Tonnetz by common tones and stepwise changes of note. Further, even though the excerpts that have been charted within these spaces (in Examples 4 and 5) are given with arrows showing the ordering of their components in time, these spaces exist inherently out-of-time. The spaces themselves do not engender any particular ordering, and can be traversed (in time) in any direction. In this respect, these musical spaces can be said to contain musical potential.

Musical substance: beyond mere potential

A spatial representation (in three dimensions) of actual rather than potential music will now be of interest. The notion of a stereoscopic score was proposed earlier, whereby the two dimensions of the standard score, pitch and time, were extended into a third dimension representing amplitude.

These three dimensions also characterize a certain mode of 3-D musical representation that I recently invoked in another study (Jones 2002), which is worthwhile to revisit here. Example 11 reproduces a passage from Iannis Xenakis's *Nomos Alpha* (1966) for solo cello, a piece that makes extensive use of unusual techniques of sound production and microtonal tuning. The last section of this example features a series of repeated notes with the indication 'fcl,' or '*frapper col legno*', meaning to hit the string with the stick of the bow instead of using the bow hair. As described in Jones (2002), the aural result of this technique depends on how

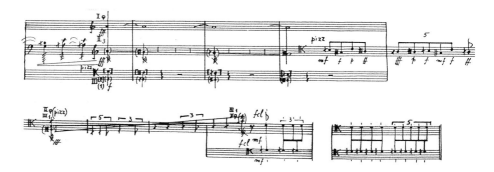

Example 11 **Iannis Xenakis, *Nomos Alpha*, page 6, lines 1–2.**

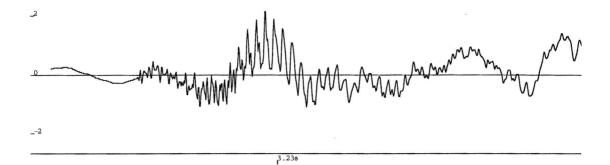

0.2

0

−2

3.23s

Example 12 **Waveform representation of second-last attack in Example 11.**

gently or aggressively the bow is made to hit the string. If the bow only taps the string gently, a high-pitched 'tap' sound results, corresponding in frequency to the distance between the bow and the bridge of the cello; if the string itself is made to rebound into the fingerboard, a much more explosive 'slap' sound results.

The passage in Example 11 is unlikely to involve any 'slaps', due to the use of the higher, tighter strings and only a moderately loud dynamic marking. But 'tap' sounds are clearly audible on most recordings: in a recording of this piece by cellist Rohan de Saram (Xenakis 1991), the tap tones in this passage begin at about E7 (four Es above middle C) and drift gradually up to G#7 (a major third higher).[10] Example 12 provides a waveform representation (drawn from de Saram's recording) of one of the 'tap sounds' at the very end of this excerpt. Time elapses along the horizontal axis, while the vertical axis represents the amplitude of the sound-wave itself – the motion of air particles. Very spiky at first, the waveform soon settles into a more broadly rolling contour, as the brief 'tap' sound dissipates.

Although this two-dimensional representation is somewhat revealing, it is very difficult to make visual judgements about frequency and timbre from its contour. A complex tone such as an instrumental timbre typically embeds many sinusoidal wave components, which are not easily seen in the waveform. These component frequencies may be separated via a mathematical algorithm known as a Fast Fourier Transform (FFT).[11] Applied to the sonic profile of a 'tap' sound from the very beginning of the section marked 'fcl' in Example 11, this algorithm generates the 3-D graph seen in Example 13. The graph charts the presence of many different frequencies (measured in kilohertz along the horizontal axis) through a brief span of time (measured in seconds along the opposing axis). The heights of the various ridges represent the amplitudes of the component frequencies. The noise of the attack can be seen on the graph at around 20 milliseconds; only a few ridges of sound persist thereafter. One ridge corresponds to the perceived 'tap' sound of E7 (2.64 kHz); another higher ridge seems to correspond to an overtone of the 'tap' sound, occurring at twice its fundamental frequency (5.28 kHz). As remarked, the 'tap' sounds in this excerpt progress up to G#7 (3.32 kHz); Figure 8 in Jones (2002) shows one ridge at this frequency and two subsequent ridges at two and three times this frequency – representing G#8 and D#9, the second and third partials of the G#7 'tap' tone.

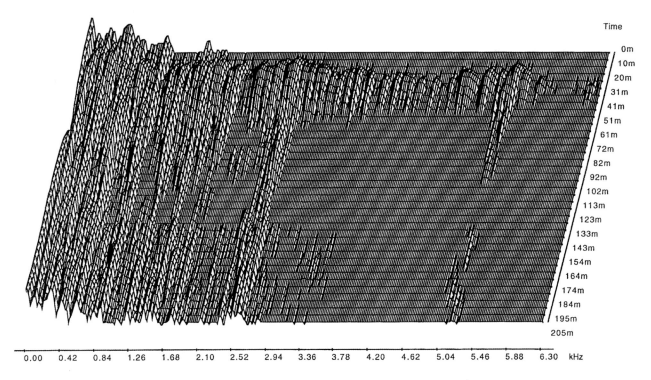

Example 13 **Fast Fourier Transform of first attack in Example 11 excerpt.**

Example 14 **Iannis Xenakis, *Nomos Alpha*, page 7, line 4; page 8, line 1.**

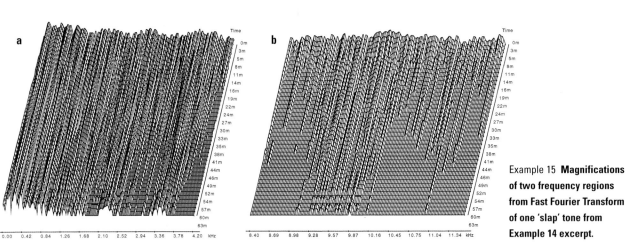

Example 15 **Magnifications of two frequency regions from Fast Fourier Transform of one 'slap' tone from Example 14 excerpt.**

Having seen so little change in frequency over the course of the graph in Example 13, we will examine FFT graphs of one additional excerpt from De Saram's recording in order to explore the temporal dimension. Example 14 provides a three-measure passage in which the cellist is instructed to effect a *col legno tremolo*, indicated by the many hatch marks below the staff. (The long notated durations would be impossible to convey with just a single strike of the bow stick.) On de Saram's recording, many of the attacks have quite a strong 'slap' component due to the loud dynamic marking and the use of lower, looser strings. Jones (2002) contains a graph (given as Figure 15b) in which the repeated *col legno* articulations can be seen as a series of parallel ridges running horizontally across the acoustic spectrum. From that figure, Examples 15(a) and (b) present two greatly magnified regions representing different areas of the FFT of a single 'slap' from de Saram's performance. Most of the noise elements in the initial attack are seen to decay quickly, especially in Example15(b). But at the very front and left of Example 15(a) are several evenly spaced spikes, which can be identified as the partials of the notated pitch. The notated piches in Example 14 are all very close to 0.12 kHz in frequency; since there are seven little spikes between 0 kHz and 0.84 kHz in Example 15(a), these spikes seem also to represent the partials of a tone or tones of 0.12 kHz. These harmonic components of the acoustic event pictured in Examples 15(a) and *(b)* are seen (and heard) to persist to a much greater degree than the noise elements at higher frequencies. Thus each of the three dimensions of these FFT graphs – frequency, time and amplitude – are seen to be of importance and relevance to a listener's impression of the musical effect.

The spatial perspective

When insight is sought into a piece of music, it proves highly useful to permit a reconfiguring of musical elements into a new geometry. Performers face the perpetual challenge of escaping from the score, transcending its literalism in some way, to achieve a level of expressiveness that the score itself cannot provide. They seek transportation for themselves and their audience – to be transported, to experience the effect of motion, energy, momentum – perhaps towards a state in which the mundane laws of Euclidean geometry no longer obtain. Music theorists also strive to motivate music, to imbue it with a certain teleology – whether in terms of the goal-directedness of the music, unfolding in time between structural nexi, or in terms of the generation of the piece from a pre-compositional seed to its fullest flowering on the printed page. Wherefore these metaphors of motion and spatiality?

Friedrich von Schelling referred to architecture as 'music in space, as it were a frozen music'.[12] And indeed music has been closely and explicitly tied to its spatial parallel discipline at least since the Renaissance, when many thinkers were described as composers, architects, mathematicians and scientists all at once.

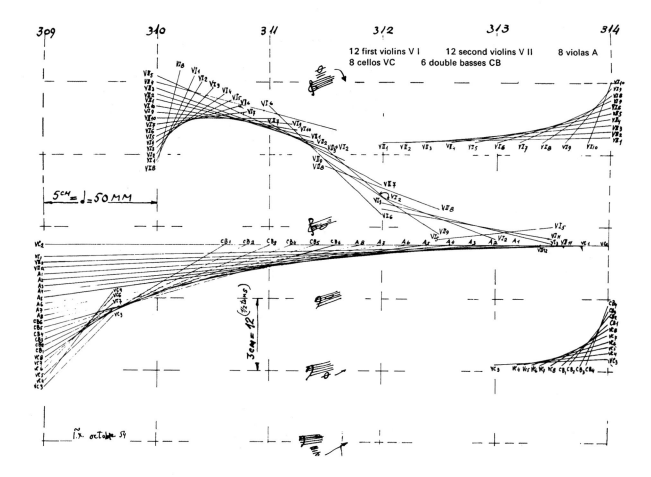

Example 16 **Iannis Xenakis,**
Metastasis, **beats 309–314.**

Guillaume Dufay's motet 'Nuper rosarum flores', composed for the consecration of the Florentine cathedral Santa Maria del Fiore in 1436, mimicked exactly the cathedral's structural proportions of 6:4:2:3 in its sectional form, and referred to the nesting of one dome inside the other atop the cathedral in a two-voice canonic setting of the chant *'Terribilis est locus'* ('Mighty is this place') (Warren 1973).

More recently, as Le Corbusier's engineer and assistant, Xenakis himself designed and supervised the construction of the Philips Pavilion at the 1958 World's Fair (Treib 1996). As shown by comparison of Examples 16 and 17, Xenakis took direct inspiration from the juxtaposed string *glissandi* in his earlier orchestral work *Metastasis* (1954) to create the strikingly warped surfaces of the Pavilion. Any separation of space and sound is, finally, untenable in the context of the staircases in the Pyramid of Kukulkan at Chichen Itza, which seem to have been designed to echo a clap of one's hands at the chirp of the Quetzal, the Mayan sacred bird (Lubman 1998). These close connections between musical and architectural

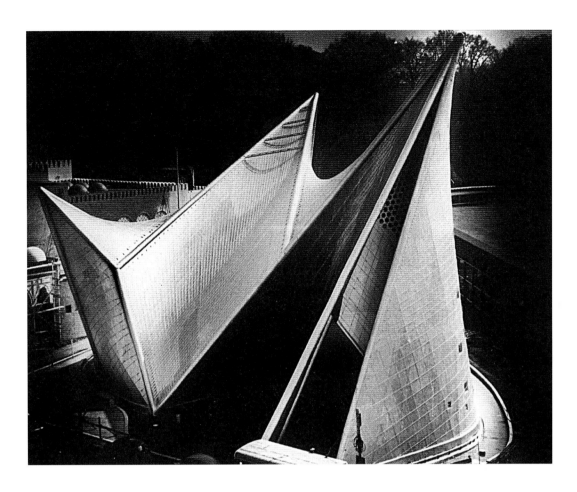

Example 17 **Philips Pavilion, Brussels World Fair, 1958.**

construction speak to the viability of the spatial perspective on musical structure.

While the traditional notation of music in a graph of frequency versus time is certainly practical and easy to read, such a representation leaves the music largely uninterpreted. A musical listener will inevitably draw all kinds of connections between different moments in a piece, in ways disproportional to the presentation of the piece in the score. It is important to find ways of reflecting our disproportional interpretation of musical structure: such spatial representations as have been examined here encourage the reconception of structural relationships in music. Moreover, a 3-D representation of musical 'space' can often provide clearer illustration of the properties of the piece or passage in question, whether simply by expanding a two-dimensional diagram into three in some way (charting time along the third axis, for example) or by considering a new musical dimension (such as amplitude). In a very real sense, then, musical cartography and artistic interpretation can be equated.

Notes

1 An orchestral score, however, groups the various parts into instrumental families rather than ordering them strictly by pitch.

2 I have not mentioned the typical disproportionality between intervals spanned in pitch or in time and their deployment in notated form. It is very common for musical spans of equal duration to be notated somewhat unevenly in terms of the lengths of the spans on the page. Further, the vertical position of a note on a staff indicates its pitch only imprecisely, since the notation of an interval does not reflect its specific size (its major or minor quality). This disproportionality distinguishes musical notation from a strictly precise graph of pitch versus time. Notwithstanding the apparent imprecision of musical notation, however, its various traditions and conveniences seem to be designed for easy reading and realization by performers.

3 Further, in any two keys a fifth apart, the unshared note in one scale will in fact be only a semitone (the minimal distance) removed from the unshared note in the other scale. Important findings along these lines have been reported by Agmon (1991), Clough and Douthett (1991), and Clampitt (1999).

4 In similar fashion, Carpenter (1988) charts the course of Brahms's *Intermezzo*, Op. 76, No. 6, and Carpenter (1997) charts the first movement of Brahms's *String Sextet*, Op. 36.

5 Equal temperament, whereby each of twelve fifths is compressed in size by one-twelfth of a Pythagorean comma, is just one of many tunings that have been used throughout history. See Jorgensen (1991) for an extensive inquiry into the history of tuning.

6 Cohn (1997) briefly outlines the origin and development of the concept of the Tonnetz but cites Mooney (1996) for a more thorough and detailed history.

7 Intervals are calculated mod 12, so that the interval from 5 to 9 is the same as the interval from 9 to 1 (both equaling 4).

8 Since graphic representations of musical structure are at issue here, it might be useful to point out the multiplicative relation that exists between the circle of chroma in Example 9 and the circle of fifths in Example 4. As shown at the bottom of Example 9, there are twelve pitches in an octave, occurring at intervals of a semitone. These twelve elements can be assigned numbers from 0 to 11 (as in Example 5). To change a semitonal circle (reading '0, 1, 2, 3, 4, 5, 6, 7, 8, 9, 10, 11') into a circle of fifths (reading '0, 7, 2, 9, 4, 11, 6, 1, 8, 3, 10, 5'), one should simply multiply every numerical element on the semitonal circle by 7 and reduce mod 12. (Note that every other element retains its original value.) Subjecting the circle of fifths to the same multiplication restores the original semitonal configuration.

9 Cohn (1997) cites Lubin (1974) as the first to recognize the toroidal geometry of the Tonnetz.

10 E7 and G#7 are examples of pitch designations established by the Acoustical Society of America. Middle C is C4.

11 With most musical instruments, the FFT reveals a spectrum of harmonics (also known as overtones or partials) sounding above a fundamental tone; their frequencies approximate the integral multiples of the fundamental's frequency.

12 See pp 576 and 593 of Friedrich von Schelling's *Philosophie der Kunst*. Also see similarly worded comparisons in Johann Wolfgang von Goethe's letter to Eckermann of 23 March 1829 (quoted in Johann Peter Eckermann's *Conversations with Goethe*), and Book IV, Chapter 3 of Germaine de Staël's *Corinne*.

References

Agmon, Eytan (1991) 'Linear transformations between cyclically generated chords', *Musikometrika 3*, pp 15–40.

Carpenter, Patricia (1983) 'Grundgestalt as tonal function', *Music Theory Spectrum* 5, pp 15–38.
 (1988) 'A problem in organic form: Schoenberg's tonal body (on Brahms's Op. 76, No. 6)', *Theory and Practice* 13, pp 31–64.
 (1997) 'Tonality: A conflict of forces', in James M Baker, David W Beach and Jonathan W Bernard (eds) *Music Theory in Concept and Practice*, University of Rochester Press (Rochester, New York), pp 97–129.

Clampitt, David (1999) 'Ramsey theory, unary transformations, and Webern's Op. 5, No. 4', *Intégral* 13, pp 63–93.

Clough, John and Douthett, Jack (1991) 'Maximally even sets', *Journal of Music Theory* 35/1, pp 93–173.

Cohn, Richard (1997) 'Neo-Riemannian operations, parsimonious trichords, and their Tonnetz representations', *Journal of Music Theory* 41/1, pp 1–66.

Cohn, Richard (1991) 'Properties and Generability of Transpositionally Invariant Sets', *Journal of Music
Theory* 35/12. pp 132.

Gollin, Edward (1998) 'Some aspects of three-dimensional Tonnetz', *Journal of Music Theory* 42/2,
pp 195–206.

Jones, Evan (2002) 'An acoustic analysis of *col legno* articulation in Iannis Xenakis's *Nomos Alpha*',
Computer Music Journal 26/1, pp 73–86.

Jorgensen, Owen H (1991) *Tuning: The Perfection of Eighteenth-Century Temperament, the Lost Art of
Nineteenth-Century Temperament, and the Science of Equal Temperament Complete with
Instructions for Aural and Electronic Tuning*, Michigan State University Press (Marquette, Michigan).

Lindley, Mark and Turner-Smith, Ronald (1993) *Mathematical Models of Musical Scales: A New Approach*,
Verlag für systematische Musikwissenschaft (Bonn).

Lubin, Steven (1974) 'Techniques for the analysis of development in middle-period Beethoven', PhD
dissertation, New York University.

Lubman, David (1998) 'Archaeological acoustic study of Chirped Echo from the Mayan Pyramid at Chichen
Itza, in the Yucatan Region of Mexico…Is this the world's oldest known sound recording?', paper
presented on 13 October at the 136th Meeting of the Acoustical Society of America in Norfolk,
Virginia.

Mooney, Michael Kevin (1996) 'The "table of relations" and music psychology in Hugo Riemann's
harmonic theory', PhD dissertation, Columbia University.

Shepard, Roger N (1964) 'Circularity in judgements of relative pitch', *Journal of the Acoustical Society of
America* 36, pp 2346–53.

Treib, Marc (1996) *Space Calculated in Seconds: The Philips Pavilion, Le Corbusier, Edgard Varèse*,
Princeton University Press (Princeton, NJ).

Vogel, Martin (1993) *On the Relations of Tone*, Verlag für systematische Musikwissenschaft (Bonn).

Warren, Charles (1973) 'Brunelleschi's Dome and Dufay's Motet', *Musical Quarterly* 59, pp 92–105.

Xenakis, Iannis (1991) *Nomos Alpha*, Montaigne Auvidis MO 782005 (Paris).

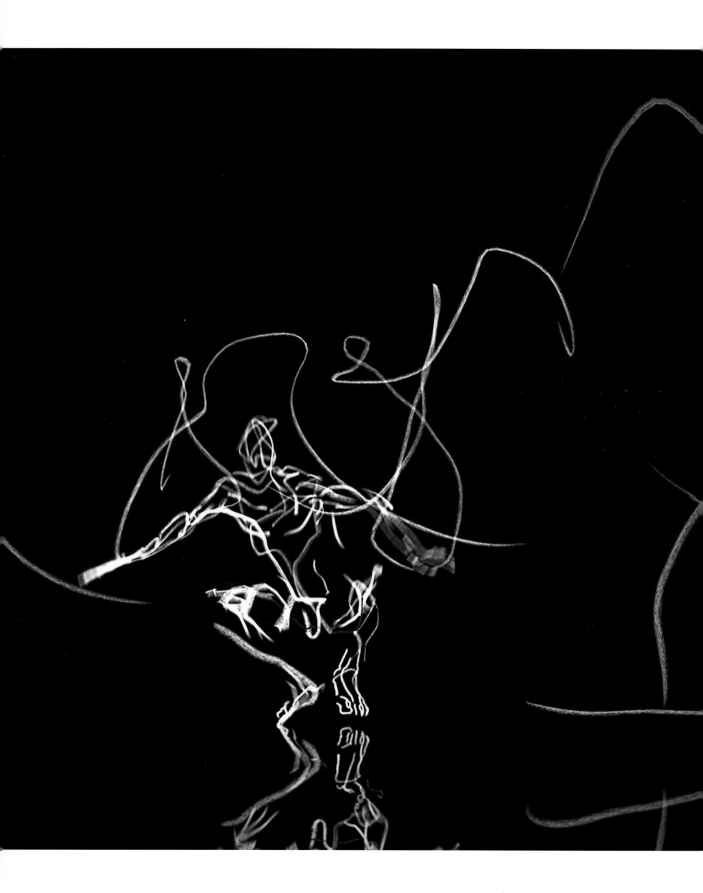

MOTION-MAPPING

Paul Kaiser

If you cast your mind back to childhood, you will soon discover our topic – motion-mapping – most clearly and imaginatively revealed. There in the games and pursuits of your earliest years you can distinguish this phenomenon in its three most basic forms. You can also follow each form forward in time to find out what they grew into – forms of art.

You might start by bringing back the movement games you played so ardently as a child – in particular the games of imitation and mimicry, like copycat, follow the leader, charades, Simon says, and the innumerable variants you would improvise with friends. These games had you map the movements of others onto your own body, sometimes in the simplest one-to-one transformations (as when you followed the leader), but sometimes more intricately, as when you mimicked a lion, or a horse, or a gladiator – or even the rain, or the wind, or an explosion. It is the rules and roles of these games that lead to choreography and dance.

Next you might summon the countless hours you spent bringing inanimate objects to life – the freest kind of play. Breaking a twig off a tree, for example, you'd make out that these little branchings could be limbs, and this little protuberance a head – and that the yard you now lay down on could be the vast world of this little creature, as you moved it about, with you its god. Make-believe of this sort points forward in many directions, from science to literature, but for our purposes let us single out puppetry and figure animation.

Now try to recall something harder to remember because it is more distant in time – perhaps most easily recovered not from memory but from observation, if you happen to have a two-year-old nearby. The activity is drawing – but drawing in its purest state, which is scribbling, where the point is not the depiction of something but rather the feeling of the motion itself and the delight at the lines of movement mapped on the paper below. This turns most obviously into the rapid marks of Zen calligraphy or of Jackson Pollock, but I also see it heading off more obscurely towards the technology of motion capture, where instead of a crayon it is a body inscribing itself not on a static piece of paper but on a flowing stream of data.

The three collaborative artworks I want to describe here all evolved, I now realize, from these deep experiences of childhood; and while my main topic is motion-mapping (as made possible by motion-capture), a second sort of mapping also figures throughout: the mapping of artistic disciplines one onto another.

OPPOSITE:
'Ghostcatching' – charcoal strokes applied and rendered.

Dance, drawing, puppetry, and film-making can be set into all sorts of reciprocal relationships when simulated – mimicked – and mapped on a PC.

'Ghostcatching', which I made with dancer/choreographer Bill T Jones and digital artist Shelley Eshkar in 1999, can serve us first by illustrating the process of motion capture and its subsequent transformations.[1] Here we can see our work illustrated in its six initial stages.

First, Bill improvised different sequences of movement according to the motifs and rules we formulated together. The reflective markers worn by him at key points of his body were all that the infrared cameras encircling the motion capture space recorded. Each camera was fed into a central workstation, which combined these inputs into a single data file.

Simple dots in 3-D space represented the motion-capture data most conveniently. These showed not the markers themselves, but rather the corresponding points in the performer's body as interpolated by the motion-capture software.

The 'biped', a kinematic model created in Discreet's character studio program, has an intricate structure of dependencies and constraints like that of the human body; like the most sophisticated marionette imaginable. But in this case the biped's motions came not from a puppeteer pulling its strings but rather from Bill dancing, for when mapped onto the biped, the motion-capture file animated it.

An alternate body made of mathematical curves (splines) was modeled in 3-D by Shelley Eshkar. The underlying biped was used as an invisible armature for this new

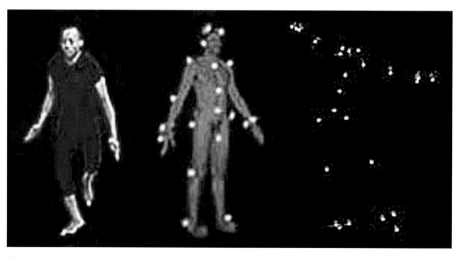

Motion capture of dancer/choreographer Bill T Jones.

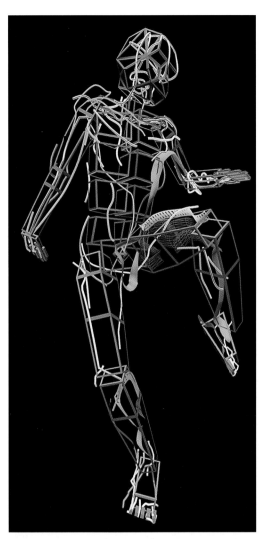

'Ghostcatching' – hand-drawn lines modeled as mathematical curves.

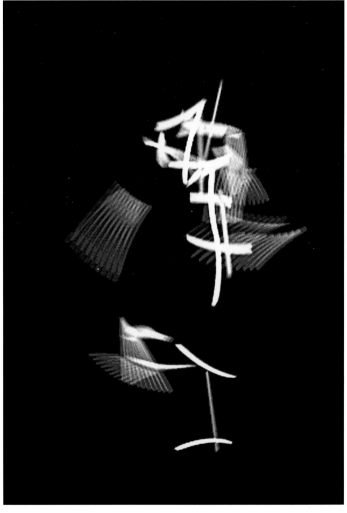

'BIPED', 1999.

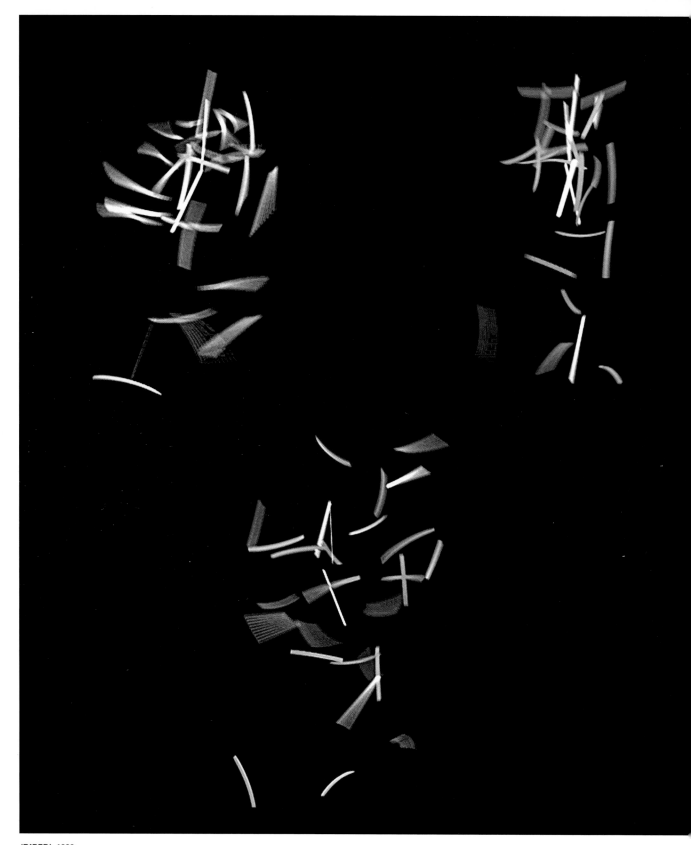

'BIPED', 1999.

body, which resembled a kind of wire sculpture. But the 'wires' were flexible, their deformations and movements tied to the underlying motions of the biped.

Sampled charcoal and other scans were texture-mapped to the splines of the new body, so that when rendered it looked like a gesture drawing – but a gesture drawing inhabiting a 3-D space and moving to Bill's dance. Each frame of the final animation was a new drawing, created by the juncture of 3-D model, motion-capture position and virtual camera viewpoint.

This, then, was our process, but to what end? The idea that Shelley and I had advanced came in part from understanding Bill's usual choreographic practice, in which he first generated new movements by dancing them himself and then set them onto the members of his company, making adjustments for their disparate physiques, styles and souls. Now we pictured Bill spinning off his movements not onto real dancers but rather onto virtual selves that we could bring to metaphoric life on the computer screen.

After studying Bill's solo dancing more closely, we asked him to isolate and intensify certain aspects of his style that we had identified. In the resulting improvisations, he danced like a man possessed – possessed in turn by eight or nine distinct selves, to whom we gave nicknames. For example there was 'Dog', whose frenetic movements were parallel to the floor and whose attention was always outward, rapidly shifting from one spot to the next. There was 'Ancestor', who cycled slowly and endlessly through six fixed poses derived from a famous set of photos Bill had made in his younger days with Tseng Kwong Chi and Keith Haring.

Bill was a bit spooked by all this, especially when his movements were first captured. He felt as if the machines were trying to steal his soul, as primitive people had first suspected photographers of doing. He said we were 'ghostcatching', which gave us our title.

The 3-D spaces that Shelley and I subsequently constructed grew entirely out of the fragments of captured movements. Around the Ancestor's fixed cycle, for example, we drew a large upright box, which contained him like a dancer's kinesphere, or a stranger's telephone booth, or a grandfather's coffin. When that figure spawned the next, breaking out of its frame, it started inscribing lines of its own, freely and ecstatically, in the surrounding space. These were the trajectories of its movement, which could be drawn not just by finger or toe but also by shoulder, or elbow, or knee. However, after a while the lines multiplied to the point where they choked off the space once more, establishing the recurring pattern in 'Ghostcatching' of being captured and then breaking free – to be captured again, and again to break free.

In our next work, we used a similar technique of mapping motion-captured dance phrases to 'hand-drawn' 3-D figures, but with several differences. First, our context had shifted: our projections now accompanied a live dance performance choreographed by Merce Cunningham, who had titled his piece 'BIPED' after the software simulation we used.[2] In our 'BIPED' stage design, we had frontal projections from the balcony hitting a transparent scrim that covered the entire front of the proscenium. This produced a strangely ambiguous perceptual zone in which our virtual figures seemed to float not only in front of the dancers on the stage, but even at times (impossibly) among and behind them. The mingling of projected figures and real dancers (never synchronized) in the same field of view made the audience ever-more conscious of our motion-mapping. Since our captured phrases were drawn from the same choreography danced on stage, the movements of our projected figures either foreshadowed or recalled those of the real dancers, depending on the order determined by Cunningham's chance operations. This was not simply a delayed visual duplication, however, for we had started to experiment more radically with our depiction of the figure, at times moving beyond the more recognizable hand-drawn forms of our previous works.

It's not that we deviated from an early decision never to distort the underlying movements we motion-captured. We knew of course that we could make a virtual figure perform impossible leaps, spins or contortions, but we had no interest in these cartoon-like exaggerations. Lost in such special effects is not only the subtlety of movement but also the crucial identification and alignment of viewer and dancer. Isn't the most important mapping in dance the imagined projection of the viewer's seated body into the dancer's moving body? For this is what transports dance beyond the visual into the kinesthetic and the proprioceptive – the audience gets into the dance not just with their eyes, but also with their flesh, muscle, bone and blood. It's like dreaming, where the body is put under the benign and protective paralysis of sleep but still shifts and twitches a bit to the tumult of mental action.

Evolution and social upbringing have made our sensitivity to human movement greater than to any other kind – the speed, intricacy and precision with which we read someone else's motion (of facial expression, hand gesture or whole body) is near miraculous. To sacrifice that intensity of perception, we had long since decided, would be foolish. But it is that very intensity of perception that can enable an odd and compelling form of abstraction. Strip the visible signs of movement to the barest of minimums, and not only will you still distinguish the walk or the run, or the leap or the tumble, but you will even still sense something of the size, the weight, the age and the intention of the body behind it.

It was this idea that Shelley and I now pursued. After the premiere of 'BIPED' in Berkeley we revised roughly a third of our sequences, shifting them towards this more minimal abstraction. Taking one of our gigantic hand-drawn figures, for example, we made it visible only in its intersection with a sparse composition of thin blue vertical lines, which lightened momentarily at the point of intersection. The almost invisible figure seemed to loom even larger this way, the physical projection filled in and somehow magnified by the viewer's interpolation.

Here we shifted not just the visibility but also the structure of our figures. Where in 'Ghostcatching' they resembled drawings of a real body, in 'BIPED' some started to look like invented anatomies, with new kinetic characteristics. These often read as figures only when set into motion. For example, one was a cluster of sticks, which were flung up into the air for a leap, then gathered back in on landing. This unreal figure didn't distort the original movement, but rather emphasized it, and the viewer never lost the sense of the actual traced body, ghost-like and invisible, moving underneath.

What we hadn't yet questioned was the hierarchy of our motion-capture interpolations. Remember that the biped simulation we were using strictly maintained the constraints and dependencies of the body. If a shoulder shrugged, then the corresponding arm and hand moved with it (the term for this is 'forward kinematics'); while, conversely, if a finger was lifted up to point at something, the elbow and the shoulder joints rotated in turn, lifting the forearm and upperarm with them (inverse kinematics). We had previously assumed that our figures should faithfully mirror or at least suggest these reciprocal linkages, which are as fundamental to the human body as they are to its simulation, but after 'BIPED' we began to wonder about other possibilities.

We soon had the ideal motion data to explore these ideas. Long having desired a lasting record of Merce Cunningham's own dancing, we had been blocked from motion-capturing him by his advanced age (he had just turned 80) and by the severe arthritis that now hobbled him. However, new advances in motion-capture technology gave us a way around this obstacle. Rather than capturing his whole body, we could now focus in on just his hands, which remained marvels of virtuosity. (Later I came across Arlene Croce's apt remark: 'Cunningham's hands are like chords of music; full articulation flows straight to the electric extremities. He

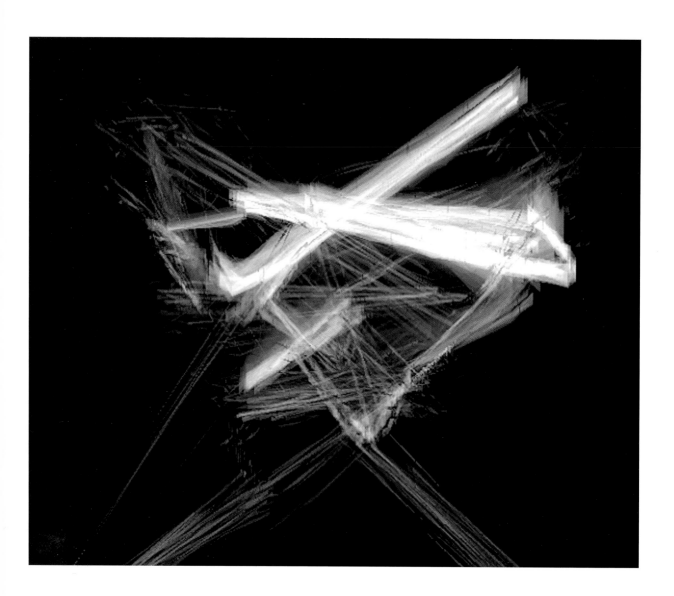

'Loops', 2000.

really does seem to have in his little finger more than most dancers have in their whole bodies').[3] Merce still performed variations on a dazzling solo for his hands, called 'Loops', which we were now able to capture.[4]

The resulting data-files tracked 21 points on each of the hands. What we now started pondering was how to connect them. Four distinct ways came to mind.

- **Anatomical:** by their hierarchical position in the hand (the default approach).
- **Proximate:** by their physical closeness to one another at a given moment in time (if one hand's thumb happened to be crossing the other hand's ring finger, then those points would be connected).
- **Cat's cradle:** by their correspondence to points on the other hand, either by direct relation (left index fingertip to right index fingertip) or by complementary relation (left pinkie fingertip to right bottom thumb joint).
- **Occlusive:** by their alignment in the z-axis (depth) in a given field of view and at a given moment of time (if one dot passed over another in a given camera angle, then both were connected).

This was exciting conceptually, but we were stuck for the moment, not having the tools at hand to create these linkages flexibly and fluidly. However, by a stroke of luck this obstacle later dissolved when we were introduced to Marc Downie, an artist and programmer in the Synthetic Characters research group of MIT's Media Lab. Marc was a masterful programmer of both artificial intelligence and real-time 3-D graphics, precisely the combination we needed. We decided to collaborate with him on a commission from the Media Lab, which was to be an abstract digital portrait of Cunningham that we also called 'Loops'.[5]

Marc proposed that we treat each motion-capture node as what he called an 'autonomous creature'. Each would 'live' digitally in a real-time 3-D world. In effect, the nodes were each to have a limited artificial intelligence, enabling them to make their own decisions about how to appear graphically, how to move in relation to their underlying motion-capture data, and how to connect to each other. They would communicate their respective states with the others, thus forming a flexible and changing network of interconnections. It was the state of this network at any given point in time that gave us our depiction of Merce's hands, one frame at a time.

'Loops' is, in effect, a live performance. It confers a weird kind of immortality on Cunningham's dance. Though it follows a 'script' (a term I use in both its film-making and programming definitions) and loops back to its beginning every ten minutes, it never quite repeats itself. Manifesting itself through the probabilistic interaction of its distinct parts, it has what is called an emergent structure, which means that it was grown as much as it was designed. Today even its creators see something new in it with every playback.

The greatest essay on motion-mapping is also the earliest I know of (I urge you to read it).[6] Written by Heinrich von Kleist in 1810 in the form of an imaginary dialogue on the marionette theater, it considers among other things the line between puppeteer and puppet. Kleist wrote that this line was nothing less than 'the path of the dancer's soul' that could be found only 'by the puppeteer transposing himself into the center of gravity of the marionette; or, in other words, by dancing'.

Our challenge now, as artists, is the same – to transpose ourselves into the vast new fields of data surrounding us, and once there, to dance.

Notes

1 'Ghostcatching', installation with single-screen color digital projection (eight minutes). Movement and voice – Bill T Jones; sound and image – Paul Kaiser and Shelley Eshkar. Opened 4 January 1999 at the Houghton Gallery, The Cooper Union for the Advancement of Science and Art. My catalogue essay, *Steps*, provides a fuller description of 'Ghostcatching' and previous works. Now out of print, it can be found on my website www.kaiserworks.com/duoframe/duosteps.htm.

2 Cunningham's familiarity with the biped figure came from his previous collaboration with Shelley Eshkar and myself on 'Hand-drawn Spaces', a three-screen digital projection, four minutes long, that premiered on 20 July 1998 at the SIGGRAPH Electronic Theater in Orlando, Florida. The new work, 'BIPED', was 45 minutes and premiered on 23 April 1999 at Zellerbach Hall, University of California, Berkeley. With substantial changes, 'BIPED' next opened on 21 July 1999 at the State Theater of Lincoln Center in New York City. A short account of 'BIPED', which I originally wrote for an Italian anthology on dance technology, may be found at www.kaiserworks.com/duoframe/duobiped.htm.

3 Arlene Croce, 'The big click', in *Afterimages* 49, Random House (New York), 1977.

4 Cunningham first performed 'Loops' in 1972 in front of a Jasper Johns painting appropriately titled 'Map' (see David Vaughan, *Merce Cunningham: Fifty Years*, Aperture [New York], 1997, p 182). Cunningham continued to develop 'Loops' over the ensuing years, right up to the time of our motion-capture session in summer 2000.

5 'Loops' was a single-screen, 10-minute installation with sound. It opened on 2 October 2001 in the group show 'Id/entity: Portraits in the 21st Century' at the MIT Media Lab. A three-screen version of 'Loops', which had two flanking screens allowing users to explore its algorithmic workings and process, opened on 25 July 2002 at the SIGGRAPH 2002 Art Gallery in San Antonio, Texas.

6 Heinrich von Kleist, 'On the puppet theater', in *An Abyss Deep Enough: Letters of Heinrich von Kleist with a Selection of Essays and Anecdotes*, trans and ed Philip B Miller, E P Dutton (New York), 1982, pp 211–16.

BELOW THE SURFACE

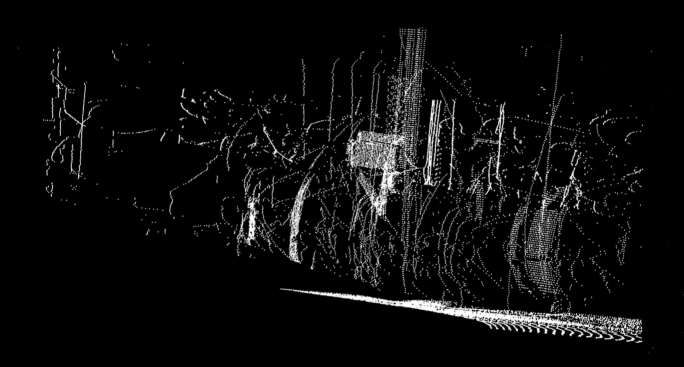

Metroscan, LIDAR point cloud of moving traffic, downtown Manhattan, Mike Silver.

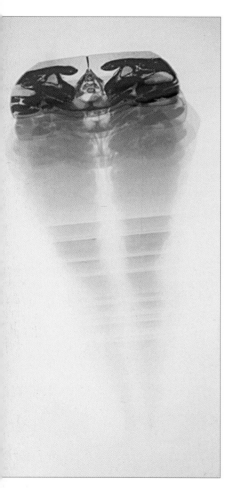  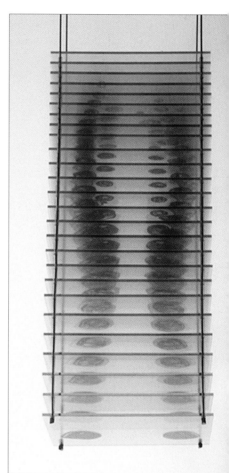

Rapt II pelvis.

RAPT

MRI Self-portraits

Justine Cooper

'Rapt: MRI Self-portraits' is a survey of the internal spaces of my body. Rapt does not simply re-present my interior anatomy; rather it constructs an alternate space through physical sculptures produced from volumetric data.

Visual explorations of the body's interior spaces constitute the historical intersection of art and science. While less invasive than traditional surgery, mapping technologies like magnetic resonance imaging (MRI) are a way of making the invisible public. Exploring the body with this new imaging tool is a clinical transgression against the physical boundaries of the individual. Contrary to the spirit of Rembrandt's famous 'Dr Tulp', the body examined in Rapt is not a corpse – it is a living body.

While X-ray machines can image the body's interior spaces they do not capture it in three dimensions. MRI scanners have the power to record spatial depth and to record volumetric data comprised of multiple slices. MRI technology works by mapping the position of hydrogen protons with magnetic energy and radiowaves. MRI machines can scan the interior of a patient point-by-point, building up a 3-D map of different tissue types.

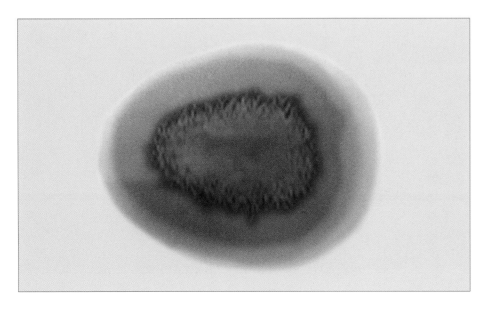

Rapt II head.

Rapt II.

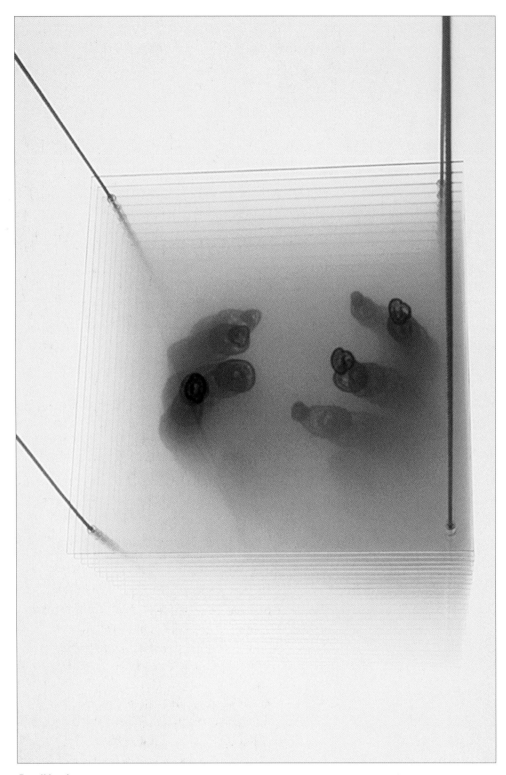

Rapt II hands.

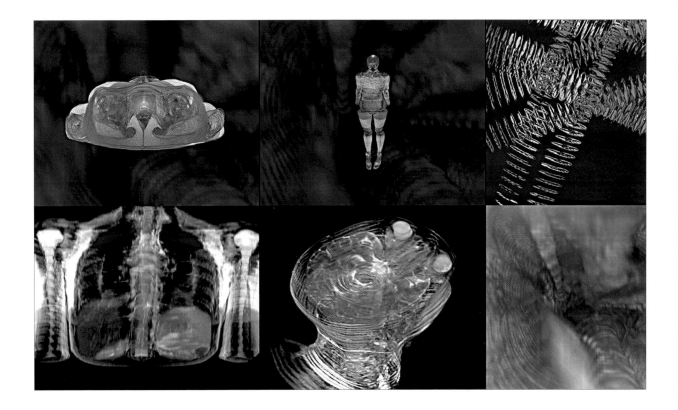

Rapt I video stills.

After setting the scanner's resolution (512 x 512 pixels) and frequency (one transversal slice every five millimeters), each section of my body was scanned separately – head, thorax, abdomen. Noises produced by radiowaves resonating within me were used as the soundtrack for a fly-through (Rapt I) generated on an SGI workstation.

An eight-meter-long body (Rapt II) was constructed from sectional data isolated with Voxelview software and printed on large Mylar sheets. Gaps in the reconstructed scan allow the viewer to pass between the slices. This is a disjointed terrain, sutured together yet still visually and experientially broken apart. A dialogue is formed between the 3-D body on a flat screen in Rapt I, and the two-dimensional stills occupying the 3-D space in Rapt II.

The serial fragmentation of the body (Rapt II) echoes the materiality lost at the moment of digitization. This is why the scans are not just a mirror of my physical presence – rather they mark the difference between lived space and represented, reconstructed space. Within art there has always been a line drawn between these two modalities.

The desire to be external to one's own form began some 5000 years ago with the invention of mirrors. Mirrors represent our desire to see the body as a representation that extends into space. For me, the doubling process can be achieved by uploading the body into a computer or by forging objects out of immaterial data.

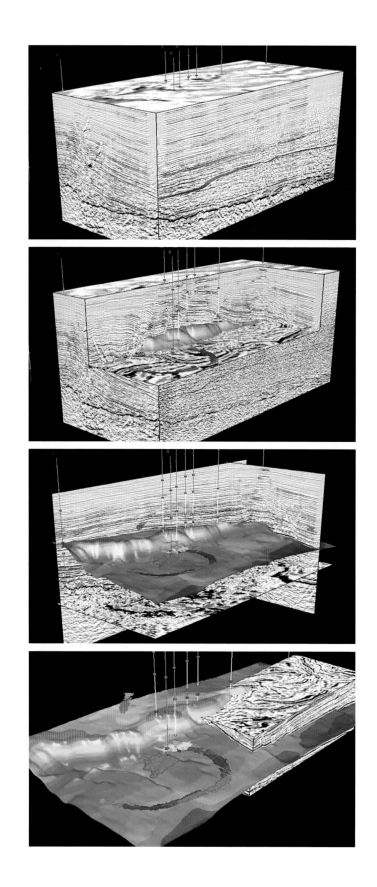

**Volumetric surveys of
subterranean space.**

Subsurface Visualization

An Interview with Duane Dopkin of Paradigm Geophysical

Mike Silver

MS: *Describe your background and how you got started. When did you begin using computers?*

DD: My interest in visualizing 3-D structures naturally began at Pennsylvania State University in the late 1970s, where a rigorous curriculum in geology both encouraged and required students to think in three dimensions. However, at this time the ability of the average geoscientist to image, visualize and model complex subsurface geological structures (for example salt domes, faults, river channels, reefs) was extremely limited and highly interpretative.

During the early to mid-1980s the seismic-imaging method that had been used successfully since the 1930s to secure two-dimensional images of the earth's subsurface was extended and enhanced so that geoscientists could secure 3-D 'reflection' images. This significant technological leap coincided with my entry into the oil industry where I began working with computer software designed to process large amounts of seismic reflection data converted into images that geoscientists could use to locate hydrocarbons found thousands of feet underground. The process of generating these 3-D images required significant amounts of computer power. Quite often, supercomputers were used to generate these images.

Although the extension of the seismic-imaging method to three dimensions had a significant and immediate impact on the oil industry, our ability to efficiently 'interpret' and exploit these subsurface images was hampered by their enormous file size. At the time, the flexibility and convenience of computer workstations, rather than the power of supercomputers, was called upon to assist the geoscientist in 'interpreting' and modeling 3-D images.

Computer software designed to interpret 3-D seismic images emerged in the early and mid-1980s and also had a significant and immediate impact on the oil industry. Early computer workstations were customized and fairly expensive, but by the 1990s general-purpose workstations and advances in 3-D graphics brought the interpretation of 3-D datasets into the hands of most exploration geoscientists. It was during the early 1990s, however, that another technological breakthrough, referred to as 'voxel-based' visualization, was introduced. Visualization based on voxels (3-D 'pixels') allowed geoscientists to literally visualize the interior of the earth and isolate complicated 3-D structures in order that they could be modeled and used as part of the oil exploration process. I was fortunate enough to be working in the company that introduced this technology to the industry. During this period I also took great interest in advancing the state of 'seismic interpretation' through the collective use of 3-D voxel-based visualization technologies with seismic transformation and imaging technologies to improve the quality and expand the information content of subsurface seismic data to reduce the risk of expensive drilling decisions.

MS: *Describe what you do at Paradigm Geophysical? What are your goals and objectives?*

DD: I am the Senior Vice-President of Technology for Paradigm Geophysical, a leading supplier of innovative 'geoscience knowledge', software technology and services to the oil and gas industry. I am responsible for overseeing the technical operation of our software solutions and ensuring that our products evolve with the changing needs of the oil and gas industry. I have the opportunity to work with some of the finest geoscientists, mathematicians and computer scientists in the world, and to witness the direct effects of their work and efforts on the world economy. My goals and objectives are quite straightforward – to provide guidance to the tremendous pool of scientific talent that are working to advance the state of seismic data-imaging and interpretation.

MS: *Describe the process of seismic data acquisition. How are the initial data obtained?*

DD: Geological structures (for example salt domes, faults, river channels, reefs) are not only three-dimensional, but frequently take on extremely complicated shapes and forms. Since many of these geological structures literally 'hold value' as 'traps' for accumulated hydrocarbons, our ability to exploit oil resources is in large part determined by our ability to image them. Accurate 3-D images of geological structures not only assist us in pinpointing the locations of hydrocarbons, they also help us understand and unravel the geological processes responsible for their formation.

Today, anyone who has traveled by air (commercial or private) can 'visualize' a modern-day geological environment and the processes that shape it. On a clear and cloudless day, we can observe the complexity of a meandering river channel, its tributaries and its flood plains from the perspective of tens of thousands of feet above the surface of the earth. These modern and dynamic depositional environments have ancient analogs that were deposited tens or hundreds of millions of years ago under similar processes and conditions. These environments, now frozen in the geological record, can be a profitable source of hydrocarbon deposits.

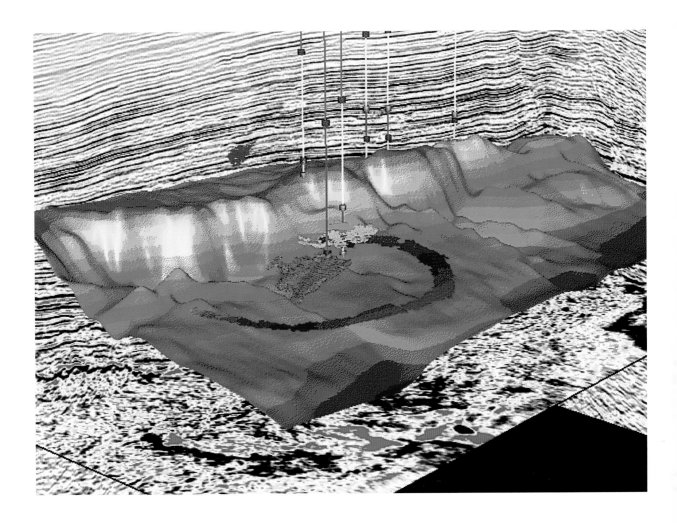

'Chair-cut' view with seismic 'interpretation' displayed in volume interior. The colored surface represents the interpreter's positioning of a significant rock boundary.

However, these ancient depositional features are obscured by younger rock formations that can be tens of thousands of feet thick. How do we find evidence of these potentially lucrative resources in the geological record?

The task of generating geologically meaningful seismic-reflection images begins with the process of 'acquiring' or collecting huge volumes of reflected 'seismic' signals. Energy initiated from a variety of man-made sources is produced on the earth's surface. This energy travels as wave fronts until they are reflected off boundaries that separate rocks with different elastic properties. This reflected energy is returned to the surface (the seismic 'response'), and recorded (by instruments referred to as geophones). Seismic data are acquired from both onshore and offshore geological basins. Today, seismic data acquisition is carried out over large areas with potentially large hydrocarbon deposits. A survey conducted in the deep-water Gulf of Mexico can cover an area of 3600 square miles and result in the recording of hundreds of gigabytes of information. Depending on the acquisition survey and parameters (number of recording instruments, number of seismic sources, recording length in time), the size of the unprocessed datasets can

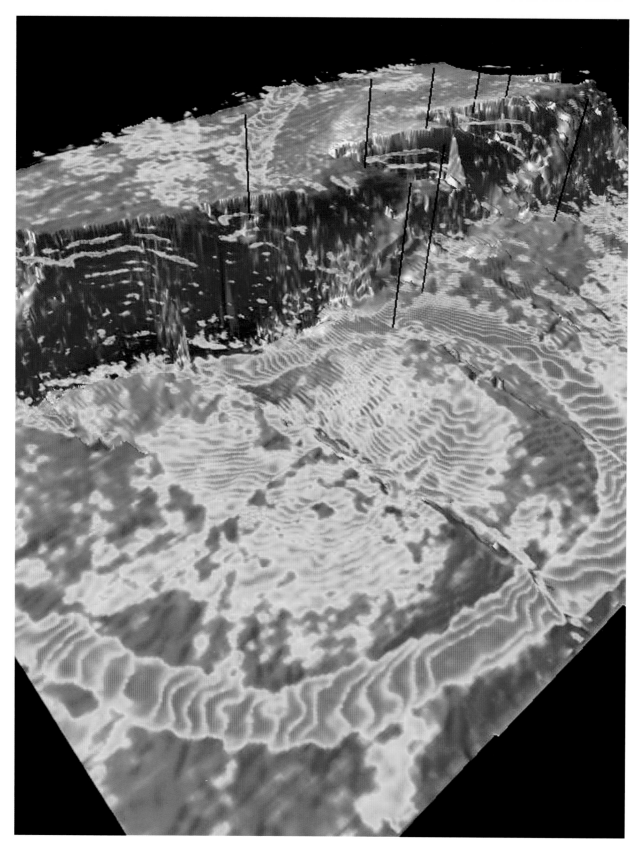

Detailed subsurface view with interpreted surfaces. This image of an ancient fluvial (river) depositional environment has modern-day analogs.

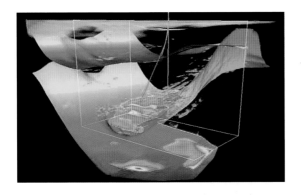

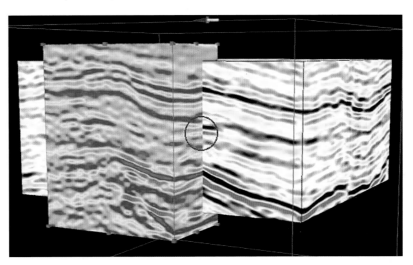

Various 3-D subsurface computer maps.

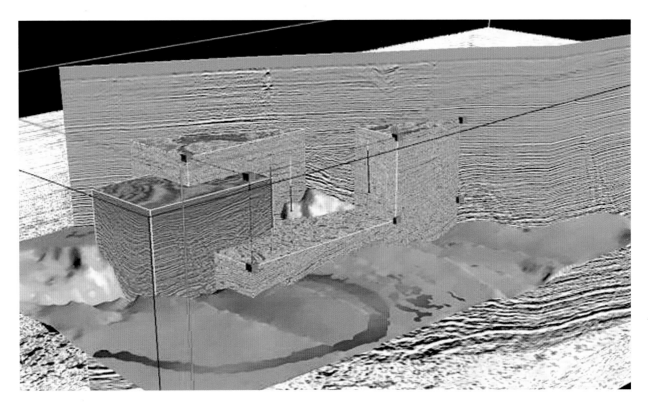

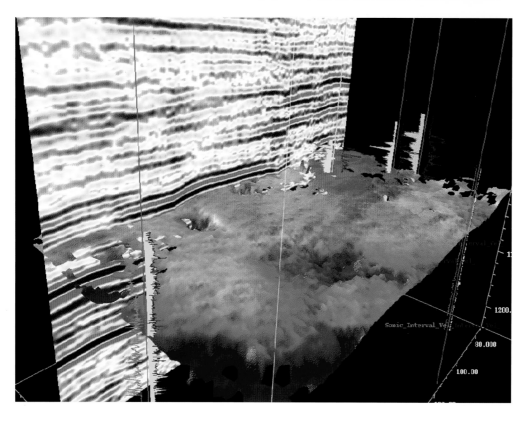

Co-visualization of seismic data, interpretation data and well-log locations.

reach into the terabytes. These data needs to be processed and reduced (compressed) to images that are meaningful to the geoscientist (seismic interpreter).

MS: *Describe the role of supercomputers in your work. How great is the speed, capacity and storage of the machines you work with?*

DD: Seismic interpretation is the science and practice of relating seismic reflections to the geology of the subsurface. Seismic interpretation is performed on high-resolution seismic reflection images, which are, in turn, generated from terabytes of unprocessed seismic field-data. The transformation of unprocessed seismic field-data into interpretable subsurface images is typically performed by applying a series of digital processes designed to remove non-reflecting energy (noise), enhance the useful seismic reflection signal, reduce (compress) the amount of seismic data and position (migrate) the reflection data to their true subsurface imaging location. All of these processes embody areas of extensive research and development with many new tools that image geological conditions. Additionally, many of these seismic processing applications are either computationally or memory intensive. Application of these processes to large amounts of seismic data requires some of the fastest and high-end computer servers available on the market today. Both shared memory (for example 64 CPUs sharing 32 gigabytes of memory) and distributed memory PC clusters with hundreds of CPUs are routinely used in the oil and gas industry to process these large volumes of seismic data. Computationally intensive processes are routinely parallelized to take advantage of these multiple CPUs. By doing so, geophysicists are able to create and deliver final image volumes to the seismic interpreter in a much shorter time. Nevertheless, it can take four to six months to transfer large seismic surveys to legible image volumes.

MS: *How is the data you work with organized and displayed? What hardware do you need to process these data?*

DD: The processed and final seismic imagery is typically a 3-D grid of signals (traces). Each trace includes the seismic response (represented as a time series of amplitudes) of many subsurface geological boundaries that separate rocks (for example sandstones, shales, carbonates) with different elastic parameters. The x and y values of this grid of seismic traces represent the actual distance or spatial sampling between trace locations (typically 12.5 meters). The z-axis is the length of the seismic signal, normally recorded and processed in 'time', reflecting the two-way journey from source to reflector (geological boundary) to geophone. Special high-end processes are needed to transform reflected time into depth, the desirable domain for seismic interpretation. This grid of seismic data, often referred to as a seismic volume, is the tool an interpreter needs to identify key subsurface features that in turn are used to generate subsurface structural maps and models.

We typically store 3-D seismic volumes as a single 3-D array of data. Each sample may be stored as 1, 2 or 4 bytes depending on the planned use for the volume. The single 3-D array may be ordered in many ways. If the intended use is processing then it is usually stored as a set of vertical slices; if the intended use is interpretation then we usually store the volume as a set of horizontal slices. If the intended use is both processing and interpretation, we store the single 3-D volume as a set of bricks that can easily be aggregated into a set of vertical or horizontal slices.

We also store interpreted horizon and fault data. If these surfaces are simple then we can store them as grids. If these surfaces are complex then we store them as a suite of grids or as a set of vectors. The speed at which complex surfaces can be created and manipulated is an area of competition for software providers in the exploration software industry.

Well data are usually stored in a relational or spatial database so that access can be limited by properties or by areas of interest. Interpreters may want to access and display the sets that penetrate a formation, the sets with auxiliary information or the sets in a specific region. Such access is best controlled with simple relational enquiries. VoxelGeo, the industry's leading voxel-based interpretation and visualization system from Paradigm Geophysical, makes great use of voxel displays, as the name of the product implies.

These displays use a different transparency value for each data value and let the interpreter see inside the volume. For example, the large negative and positive values might be set opaque and all other values set transparent. This would allow the interpreter to see 'bright spots' (large values) exclusively. These bright spots are common indicators of gas since subsurface gas generates a strong soundwave reflection. Other settings like opacity can accentuate a variety of subsurface features. We can choose to visualize discontinuities that may be faults or the banks of a channel. The choice of opacity settings depends on the interest and skill of the interpreter. These displays are generated by modern 3-D graphics hardware by texture rendering the 3-D volume.

MS: *What has been the impact of voxel-based visualization technology on the process of locating hydrocarbon deposits? Are there real benefits in using this system? If so, what are they and who profits?*

DD: The interpretation process is fairly systematic. The geoscientist identifies key geological features or rock boundaries (horizons) on a gridline-by-gridline basis and then attempts to integrate the results with data obtained from other 'line interpretations'. The problem with this approach is essentially twofold: firstly, geological features are complex and 3-D, and interpreting seismic data along parallel lines that intersect complex structures can be quite misleading; secondly, seismic volumes can be quite large with thousands of lines running in two mutually perpendicular directions, so a detailed geological interpretation of such large volumes can take months.

Voxel displays have revolutionized 3-D seismic interpretation. Bright spots or indicators of gas can now be seen and interpreted directly from the volume. Previously they were interpreted from amplitude maps extracted from fully interpreted horizons. One of the maxims of historical interpretation was to pick out a depth section and map the extent of an anomaly in space. With 3-D opacity displays we can clearly see the extent of the anomaly in depth and space.

The ability to see channels, fans, point bars and other depositional features first before any conventional picking and mapping is performed is a great enhancement to interpretation. These features have characteristic shapes and can be recognized immediately by an interpreter or geologist. Once the feature is recognized, the interpreter can guess the nature of potential reservoirs and where the sand concentration is likely to be greatest. The interpreter can also decide on the best way to map this feature. The visualization provides the answer first then lets the interpreter fill in the details. In conventional interpretation the order is reversed. Detailed picking and map-making would gradually reveal the answer if pursued to completion. The improvement is great to a skilled interpreter.

The benefits of this technology largely accrue to oil companies and are passed onto the general public in the form of reduced finding costs for oil. The reduction of finding costs is largely a reduction of the energy used in drilling. The increased success of wells and the reduction of dry holes is another benefit.

MS: *What part of the Yale Symposium on Digital Mapping intrigued you the most? Whose work did you consider useful in your area of research?*

DD: What interested me the most were the fundamental needs and similarities across the disciplines (arts, sciences and engineering) when it came to the modeling and representation of 3-D structures. I was most intrigued by the similarities of some of the fundamental principles of seismic imaging and 'energy mapping' as presented by Eric Heller. Both sciences employ ray- and wave-based theory to generate images, and both deal with the issues of representing complex ray phenomena such as caustics.

TRACES AND SIMULATIONS

Mike Silver

The following projects explore two types of maps: traces and simulations. The difference between the two is primarily a function of time. Traces report on conditions as they are or have been while simulations anticipate future events by modeling known processes. Technologies like light direction and ranging (LIDAR) can record large three-dimensional objects at very high-resolutions. What gets recorded is confined to the visible surface of a scanned object. The software for the Baptistry was designed to map space in depth, setting up complex relationships between neighboring cells in a turbulent web of calculations. Here, the interaction between building and landscape produces a traversable ground, the appearance of which is determined by the cloudlike and turbid flow of materials moving above and below the surface. In the Liquid Crystal Glass House, space is created by the interactive exchange between bodies and architecture. While the first three projects here are surface-to-surface translations that exploit new techniques of mapping, the last two form networks that join events and entities together in four dimensions.

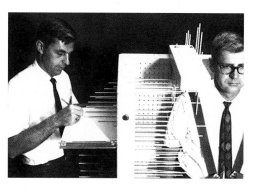
Manual body-mapping technique.

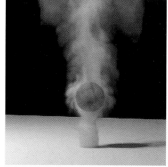
Flow simulation around a sphere.

The post proportional body

Most 3-D scanning devices measure the reflection of laser light, bouncing off an object or body. Some technologies utilize an automated sensor or haptic probe to generate 'maps', while others employ the distortion of optically projected patterns used to digitally interpolate non-regular 3-D surfaces (moiré phase shifting).

Given the power and speed of today's computers an extremely dense collection

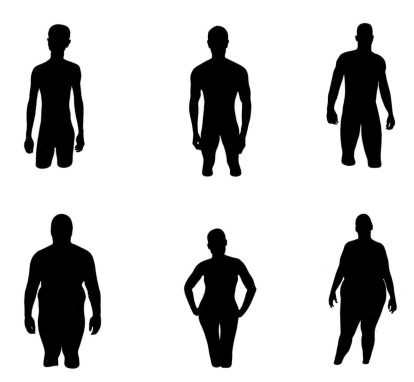

The post proportional body.

of measured points can be stored, manipulated and displayed. These 'soft' carto-graphic technologies accommodate irregular forms that cannot be conventionally described by ideal geometries, linear perspective, flat photographs or paper maps.

By abandoning the tendency to generalize reality, digital mapping technologies undermine the role ergonomic surveys play in the measurement of organic bodies. These new techniques of space mapping challenge two seemingly fundamental assumptions about the relationship between the body and architecture. The first is that a building's proportions must by necessity base themselves on stand-ardized dimensions culled from the survey of a limited human population. The second assumption maintains the belief that these measurements should be organized for aesthetic reasons according to the logic of a pre-established algorithm.

By linking proportional harmonies like the Golden Section with attempts to stand-ardize anthropomorphic measurement, a system such as Le Corbusier's 'Modular' perpetuates the formation of a normative order while in the same turn reinforcing our tendency to search for relationships that conform to an abstract mathematical rigor. The Modular was therefore based on a twofold prejudice: first that a normal body actually exists, and second that its dimensions should be organized according to an *a priori* mathematical order.

While our current preferences for size, shape and weight may have changed our dependence on standards has not. A 'post proportional' body on the other hand exists without a specified mass, regularity or standardized appearance. It is not an average body – it is everybody.

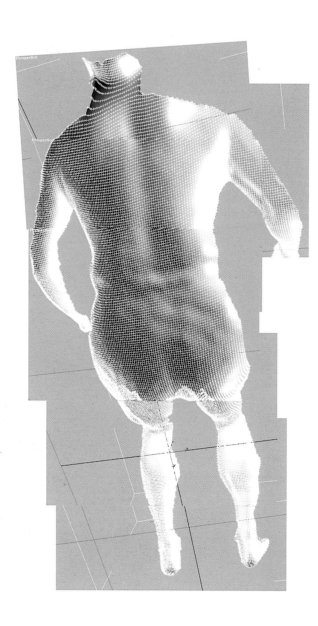

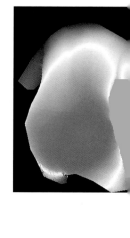

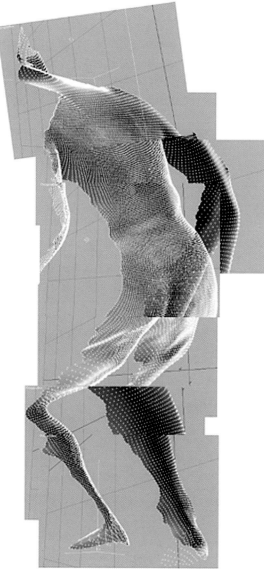

**Rendered body scans of data obtained
from Inspec's 3-D optical scanner.**

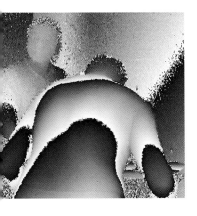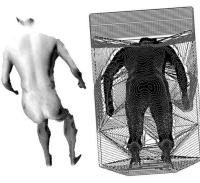

Non-ideal systems of measurement based on soft cartographic technologies allow us to reconsider the long-standing practice of organizing the world according to a precalculated framework of dimensions inherited from narrow surveys of military personnel, ergonomic charts and industrial standards. The so-called imperfections, which distinguish good forms from bad, and the differences that do not follow pre-established standards, can be imaged and robotically materialized in ways unthinkable only a decade ago.

In this scenario, the idea of deviance disappears along with preconceptions about what constitutes the normal body. Here notions of physical health (properly the subject of medicine) are detached from bodily images circulated in the media and supported by historically narrow aesthetic criteria. A person can be overweight and at risk of a heart attack while at the same time perceived as physically desirable, just as fashion models are considered attractive even though they may be anorexic.

With new techniques of digital mapping and fabrication, the benefits of customized tailoring can be mechanized allowing for the robotic production of a large differential series. For the Portrait Chair project, a 3-D optical scanner (designed to map live bodies) was used to build furniture that precisely fits the contours of a single user. For the final chair (made from recyclable materials), data from the scanner were sent to a large CNC mill. In this way the project demonstrates an efficient method for mass-customizing marketable products from digitally acquired, site-specific spatial data. No standard of average ergonomic data is put forward as the driving geometry for the chair.

Chair fabrication process from optical scanner to CNC mill tool paths to final product.

Salvage House prototype

The Salvage House was designed from the discarded remains of obsolete military aircraft. Components recycled into the house subvert the logic of war by reprogramming its artifacts. 'Turning swords into plow shares', the project works against neofuturist attempts to aestheticize the relationship between 'War and Architecture'.[1] Avoiding the scars, breaks, and violent juxtapositions commonly found in both ad hoc and surrealist art, the goal was to use digital technologies to produce a new formal language, one that can anticipate integrated structures not dependent on an articulated collision between two or more parts. For the house, a

Salvage House rendering.

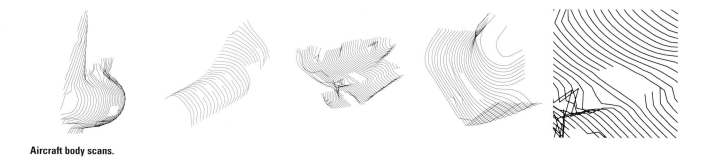

Aircraft body scans.

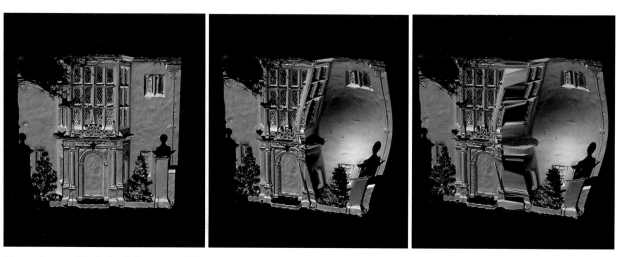

Distorted scans of Berkeley College master's house.

simple process of bilateral duplication or 'mirroring' generates a wholeness that is both unfamiliar and new. Different schemes for the house were explored by carefully doubling point cloud files stored in a database of 3-D aircraft body scans. Through digital mapping technologies, a wide range of strategies could be tested prior to refinement of the project.

Casting shadows: LIDAR signal processing and noise

The Yale Archives was designed using high-resolution 3-D laser scans of existing classical ornament found on site. Unable to capture the undercuts and crevices of these complex details, the scanner instead generated a series of fragmentary traces. This effect is produced by the reflection of laser signals as they illuminate and record their target. Like a bright spotlight, LIDAR machines cast shadows that are visible in the computer as a series of irregular holes. Surfaces running parallel to the laser also produce a set of random breaks gathered along the edges of a scanned object.

The intrinsic plasticity of LIDAR data permits its facile manipulation. With a simple algorithm points selected from the scan were projected into an ellipsoid and then flattened out. This was done to accentuate the tears generated during the mapping process and to make them easy to fabricate with the dual-axis feature of a large-format CNC wire-cutter. (The manipulated scans created both a flattened elevation of the original ornament as well as a complex ruled surface that can be easily made into digitally cut foam molds for poured-in-place concrete.) Through 'explosive projection', the distortion of small details became the seeds for a full-scale building.

Unlike the Salvage House or the Portrait Chair projects, this work explores the active transformation of data as it moves between media operating in specific

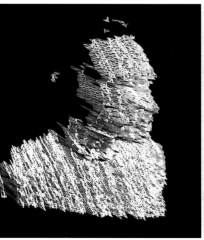
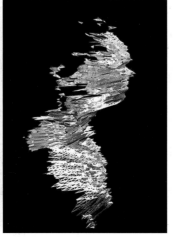
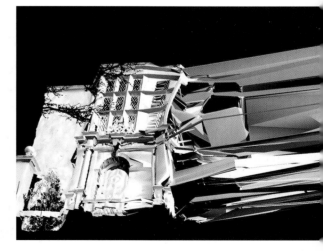

LIDAR scans with noise.

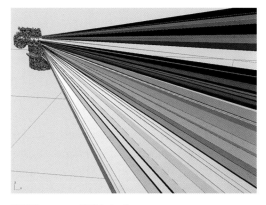

LIDAR scanner, CNC hot-wire
foam cutter and ruled surface
generated from scanned data.

Explosive Projection algorithm
used to translate noise and
surveyed data into a form
compatible with the cutter.

situations and at different times. The absence displayed by the trace is not an error that is 'corrected' or ignored. What is lost becomes stretched, amplified and remapped, making the process productive as well as reflective. The Ionic capital, produces its own mutation as it travels from the world through the computer and back again. The resulting architecture becomes as much a device for the reception of data contaminated by 'noise' as it is the transmitter of a new message. In this way matter and information become as inseparable as form and content.

Scripts, networks and cellular automata

The interior envelope of the Liquid Crystal Glass House consists of a faceted metal cage covered with liquid crystal glass panels. Each panel operates in concert with its neighbor to form a responsive system of electronic surfaces open to constant adaptation and change. Switch-like partitions, doors, and door locks responding to movements inside the house, control appropriate levels of exposure, privacy and sun protection. Areas of opaque (or transparent) glass can in this way be materialized on demand, dissolved away in an instant or shifted between different zones in space.

While the interaction between walls and switches in the house is both scripted and fixed, (see www.vrlglass.net) the fenestration patterns initiated by their exchange are not. Using cellular automaton (CA) programs, complex self-organizing geometries based on simple rules are played out over the lifetime of the project. The ultimate configuration of these window patterns is unpredictable because their continuous iteration does not always settle into routines that can be predicted in advance. The only way to know how the windows will behave is to set them in motion.

Linking domestic life with cellular automaton programs embedded in the computational structure of the house is one way of making 'literal transparency' and opacity the binary code that supports emergent phenomena and self-organizing complexity. In this way the house forms a constantly changing feedback loop sustaining four-dimensional interactions that relate in endless and unpredictable ways.

VRML Simulator, interior of liquid crystal glass shell and switching diagrams.

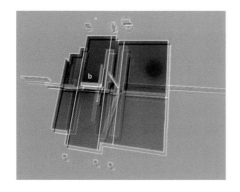

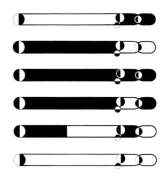

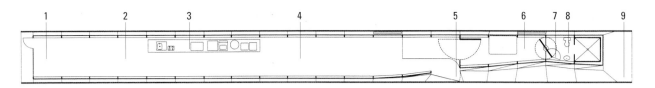

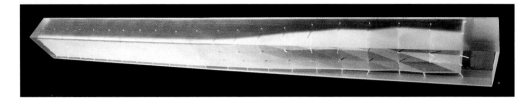

House model.
1. Study
2. Dining room
3. Kitchen
4. Living room
5. Entrance
6. Bedroom
7. Entry vestibule
8. Bath
9. Garden/veranda

Unfolded glass shell with cellular automaton fenestration pattern.

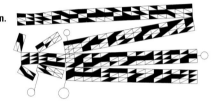

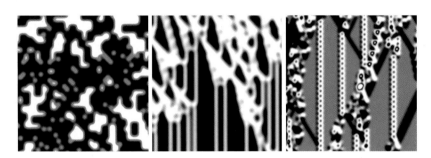

Cellular automata.

OPPOSITE:
Flow animations (movie stills).

Computational fluid dynamics

Tidal basins are formed in coastal areas by the ebb and flow of the sea. Characterized by the intermittent presence of shallow water and semi-dry land, these constantly changing landscapes are traditionally considered unsuitable for the building of permanent structures. At low tide the bay of Mont-Saint-Michel appears as a great expanse of mud and wet sand stretching for miles along the Normandy coast. The Baptistry was designed for this unstable terrain, harnessing its periodic transformation as a way against the static monumentality of conventional architecture.

Parishioners visiting Mont-Saint-Michel gain access to the Baptistry along the island's eastern edge. At low tide the project acts as a vessel containing baptismal pools of salt water. These pools are filled up when the building disappears. While submerged, the intended use of the Baptistry is temporarily preserved without its visible presence. The project underwater continues to function because its purpose is fulfilled by the sea. In this way architecture oscillates between consecrated ground experienced as a local condition, and concerted ground dissolved into the boundless expansion of space. The function of the site is everywhere – the world becomes a building.

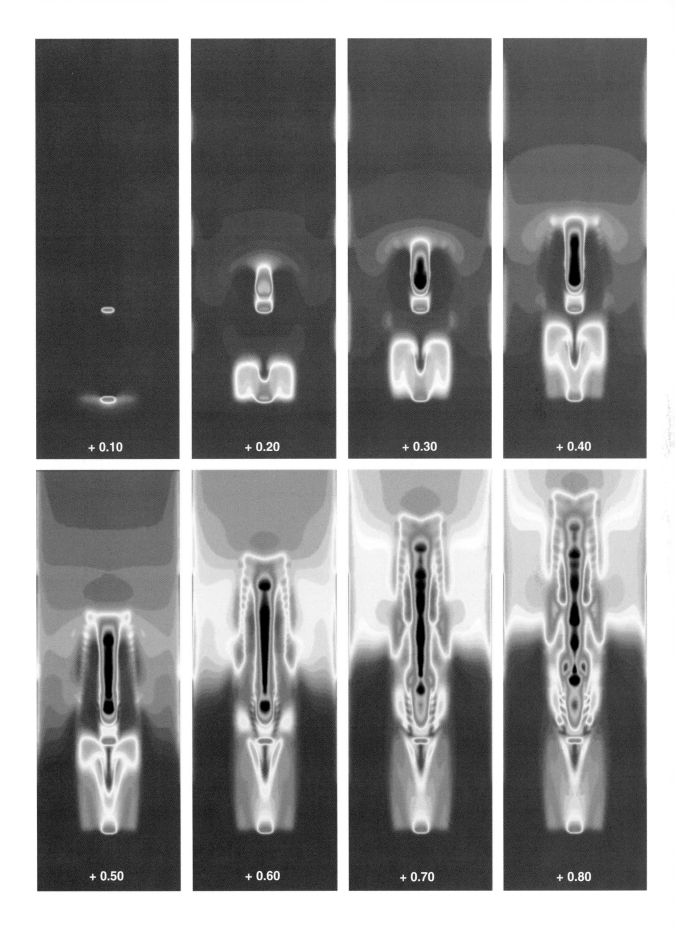

+ 0.10

+ 0.20

+ 0.30

+ 0.40

+ 0.50

+ 0.60

+ 0.70

+ 0.80

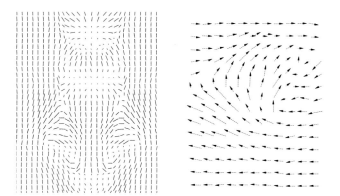

Vector maps.

At low tide the Baptistry acts as a channeling device that both harnesses and reconfigures the landscape. An uneven stretch of semi-dry earth used as a staging area for church-sponsored events is produced by the outward rush of seawater. In this way, alluvial structures formed by sediments flowing around stationary objects are endlessly produced on site. Pools of water trapped in this landscape are employed for ceremonial purposes (as fonts).

A physics-based flow simulator was used to anticipate the magnitude and shape of this newly deposited land. Water velocity, silt density and composition were fed into a program written by Flow Analysis Inc. The software (originally designed to replace wind-tunnel experiments) functioned in this project as a design tool. The surface generated by the interaction between building and land-scape can be understood in section as a relatively deep space that has a direct influence on appearances above ground.

In this sense architecture is defined by the flow generated between a solid yet programmatically incomplete form (functioning like the spoiler on the wing of an aircraft) and the constantly surging geomorphology of the site. Here the rigidly ordered laminar flow of water and sand gives way to complex self-organizing vor-tical structures that eventually dissipate in a random form of turbulence. Functional requirements are served not by static elements placed on a site, but by networked iterations. In the simulation, subtle changes of the spoiler's design, i.e. different notch and corner dimensions, produced vastly different flow config-urations (Figure c, opposite).

Notes 1 Neal Leach, *The Anesthetics of Architecture*, Verso Press (London), 1997, p 11.

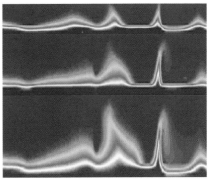

a.

b.

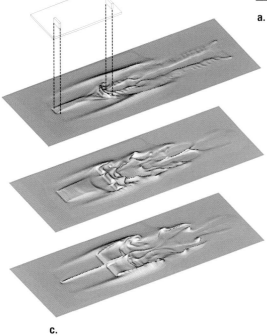

a. Section of flow simulation model by William
   Dietz of Flow Analysis Inc.
b. Landscape transformation.
c. Different flow simulations generated from
   small changes in building details (simula
   tion model by William Dietz of Flow
   Analysis Inc).
d. Isosurfaces (fonts).
e. Plans.

c.

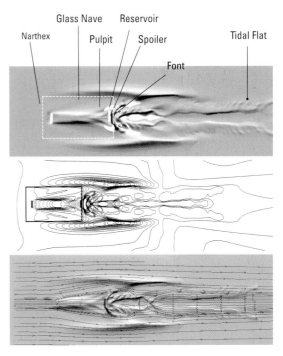

Narthex   Glass Nave   Reservoir
           Pulpit   Spoiler
                      Font   Tidal Flat

d.

e.

Voxels

An Interview with Julie Dorsey of Yale University

Mike Silver

Simulated weathering.

MS: *How did you get started in computer graphics research?*

JD: As an undergraduate I studied architecture. I was also very interested in computer science and mathematics. When I wandered into the computer graphics department at my university to ask a professor some questions I was fascinated by the various graphical displays in the lab. Though I saw just a tiny glimpse of the field that day, it immediately appealed to me as a way to bring my interests in architecture and computer science together.

Most of the research I've done focuses on problems addressing the design and visualization of the built environment. I have found that work in one area has often led to insights in another. Much of my research has been focused on interconnected concerns.

MS: *At the Yale Symposium on Digital Mapping you presented a series of images that showed the computer simulation of weathered and eroded solids. What led you to this research?*

JD: In my PhD thesis I developed a computer-graphics system for the design and simulation of opera lighting and projection effects. A simulation for the opera *La Boheme* that I worked on in 1991 is still considered by many to be a state-of-the-art example of photo-realistic image synthesis, though it pales in comparison with the real scene built on-stage. My simulation looked too perfect; it lacked the wear and tear that is so important for establishing the ambience of a scene. Unfortunately the material models widely used in computer graphics assume that materials are both pristine and immutable, even though real materials are neither. After the opera project, I started to look at the problem of developing models of materials that can change over time, and simulating some of the processes that generate different appearances.

MS: *Can you explain the differences between standard surface models and volume-based object representations? What kinds of simulations would the latter permit?*

JD: Geometric models in computer graphics are generally represented as either

surfaces or volumes. Surface representations are more prevalent because they offer a number of advantages. Since most objects are opaque, all the information necessary to render them is usually associated with their visible skin. For instance, attributes like colors and reflectivity are often sampled into texture images that are simply painted on the model. Among the many types of surface representations, triangle meshes have the advantage that they can be directly processed by today's graphics hardware. Surface representations can be locally deformed by simply modifying control points. However, such deformations generally fail to account for the internal physical properties of the model, and can create self-intersections that are difficult to detect or prevent. In addition, performing topological changes to the model, such as drilling a hole through it, is challenging using just a surface description.

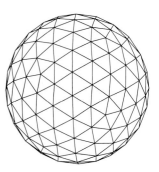

Mesh model.

Volumetric representations encode not only the surface of the model but also its interior. Many volumetric representations are based on a 3-D grid, for example voxels store a binary occupancy value at each vertex. Many schemes reduce storage costs by storing samples within a hierarchical structure instead of a single, uniformly sampled grid. Generally, representations based on 3-D lattices are more costly to render, since they must be either ray traced or converted into a surface. Additionally, deforming a volumetric model is difficult since it involves expensive shifting of data over cell boundaries. Three-dimensional grids differ from surfaces in that they support robust sculpting operations and other deformations that affect the internal structure of the model.

The optical properties of volumetric representations are also important. Surprisingly, the physical basis of reflection for many materials does not result from the interaction of light with the surface itself, that is, the infinitesimal interface

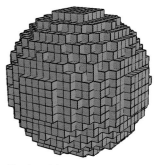

Voxel model.

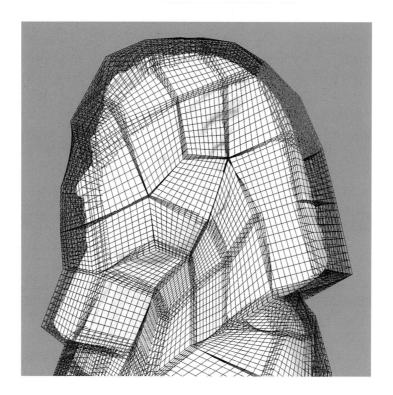

Volumetric skin divided into sectors (voxels).

between the air and the media, but rather from inside the material. This phenomenon is called subsurface scattering, and is common in organic forms such as vegetative and animal matter, as well as dielectrics such as plastic and other composite materials. In subsurface reflection, light is transmitted across the interface into the material media. Once inside the media, light is scattered and absorbed by the constituents of the media. (This process is similar to how light might interact with a cloud of water vapor.) Light that is scattered may eventually exit the media, and to the observer it appears as reflected light.

The theory of scattering from a layered media was originally developed to explain radiative transport in planetary and solar atmospheres but has also been further developed by researchers interested in the appearance of paint, skin, vegetation and the ocean. My colleagues and I have been developing computer models of subsurface scattering in order to simulate the interaction of light with skin and stone.

MS: *Texture mapping has become the standard way to render material surfaces in a realistic way. When voxels are used the surface actually grows – it is not merely a projection made on an infinitely thin membrane. Something like a second skin begins to form. Rather than just a visual affect you have here the beginnings of a system that can map or simulate the behavior of material accretions and chemical change acting in 3-D space. Entropic processes like erosion and breakage can be simulated along with the creative growth and transformations of patinas and stains. The ultra-clean, dust-free surfaces produced by current visualization software hark back to the early Modernist obsession with whiteness, hygiene and purity. Do you see this as something facilitated by the immateriality of information? Is it the result of cultural preferences or the limits of our current tools?*

JD: I think that the pristine look of today's computer renderings is really a result of technical limitations, rather than cultural preferences. As the ability to visually model a wide range of surfaces develops, it will be interesting to see what designers do with this. One could imagine the design of new appearances that have never been seen before. Clearly this could have a big impact on the field of architecture.

MS: *Can these visualization tools be used to predict how the environment will affect a real building over time? Can the vicissitudes of place be factored into a simulation?*

JD: The complex mechanisms of weathering – for example the flow of water, effects of ultraviolet radiation and so on – are not fully understood based on first principles; the state of our scientific knowledge is incomplete. But even if we had exact knowledge of these mechanisms, the complicated microscopic and macroscopic heterogeneities of the material's interior, and the variability of climates in which an object is placed, it would still be impossible to describe the process of weathering in full detail.

Subsurface scattering: light passing through a volumetric model.

While the experimental data to support a physical simulation that would predict the appearance of a material are not available, we have begun to develop a series of phenomenological models to simulate some of the processes that affect appearance, based on the best available evidence. In one project we modeled the development of metallic patinas. Here we used data from the corrosion literature that describe the varying compositions of patinas in different environments. We used this information to simulate the range of appearances that occur among marine, rural and urban environments.

I believe that these techniques have many applications in computer graphics, even if they do not perfectly predict real physical processes. By varying the shape of objects – indeed, just being able to do this at all – the material properties and the initial conditions of the simulations, we can create strikingly different effects that move beyond the polished appearances that have limited the range of effects that we could simulate on computers.

MS: *Do you see your work as addressing concerns outside of those dominated by special-effects artists to include more pragmatic disciplines? If so what would they be?*

JD: Definitely. As we gain insight into the structure of materials and develop new computer models, they will be able to benefit a host of new design and engineering applications. For example, automobile designers might study various coatings applied to virtual car models in order to understand the structure, appearance and performance of coatings over time. Architects and conservators might be able to model the long-term durability of material components or conservation treatments. Finally, computer models of materials could give rise to the design of entirely new appearances. Although the inherent complexity of materials makes developing models extremely difficult, the strong physical basis of the new models makes them potentially suitable for these and other applications.

MS: *What part of the Yale Symposium intrigued you the most?*

JD: I liked the visualization of large-scale geological structures, as it made clear the importance of being able to model extremely large subsurface structures.

MS: *The interest in folded space and curvilinear surfaces fits well with the way available software technology could model architectural space. In the 1990s we saw a productive convergence of theory and technology that generated limits serving a specific architectural agenda. Do you see this alliance as something that can continue to produce new innovations in architecture? If so, can we imagine something beyond the surface, something that grows out of a sense of depth and volume? Do you see future increases in speed and computing power as a way of shifting visualization technology away from surface effects, for example texture maps, meshes and lofted nurbs, to a voxel-based modeling paradigm where outward appearances are intimately linked to the volumetric structures that compose them?*

JD: Yes, I think people are just starting to understand the potential of being able to model the interior of complex shapes. I actually think that what we're likely to see is new hybrid data structures that begin to combine some of the advantages of surface- and volume-based representations. Many real-world objects have complex, often layered geometries and compositions that are not well represented by either

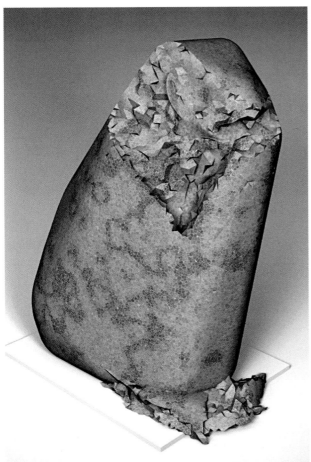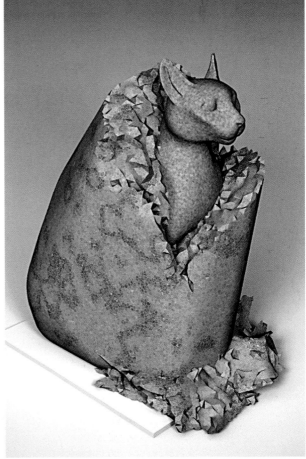

Voxel model using tetrahedral mesh.

surfaces or volumes. The photograph opposite shows two images of a stone sculpture taken sixty years apart. It is notable from this example that the shape and appearance of an object are often the result of complex physical processes or human intervention. While there has been tremendous progress in modeling and 3-D acquisition techniques in the last few years, these techniques are geared towards producing surface models at a fixed point in time and are not well-suited to this class of objects.

We are developing a new geometric representation that consists of layered tetrahedra, and combines the qualities of both surfaces and volumes. Tetrahedral representations can accurately capture both a visible external surface as well as the hidden interfaces between material layers. Because its surface is simply a triangle mesh, the model appears externally like a traditional surface representation, thus it can accurately model sharp features like creases and corners. Moreover, the surface triangles can be texture mapped and rendered directly by the graphics hardware. Within the interior, the tetrahedra offer the flexibility of a volume. Topological changes are performed by simply removing or splitting tetrahedra. Unlike grid-based volumes, tetrahedral models can be deformed easily by moving their vertices, in applications such as freeform deformation or finite element method (FEM) simulation. Such simulations accurately reflect the behavior of the solid, if one is careful to keep the tetrahedra well proportioned.

MS: *Has any of this technology affected other disciplines? If so, which ones?*

JD: The medical profession has been working with volume models for decades now. They've developed a variety of techniques for taking data acquired through magnetic resonance imagers (MRIs), for example, and converting it to volumetric representations that can be examined and probed with computer graphics.

OPPOSITE:
Simulation of surface erosion and staining.

CONCLUSION

Historical Perspectives on Representing and Transferring Spatial Knowledge

Denis Cosgrove

Our understanding of the history of maps and mapping – of 'cartography' to use a nineteenth-century neologism – has been revolutionized over the past quarter of a century. The shifts are as profound as those in map-making and the use of maps resulting from satellite remote sensing, digitized spatial knowledge for geographical information systems (GIS) and computer imaging. Three of the principal shifts in cartographic historiography are worth highlighting here.

First, there has been detailed exposure of the ideological power of maps and the active roles they have played in the nexus of power-knowledge framing and shaping of the geographies of the modern world. Geographic and topographic mapping and maps played a central role not only in the Western colonization of territories, peoples and the natural world but have also been critical tools for the modern state and its agencies in shaping social and moral spaces.

Second, map-making's scientific claims to offer accurate and objective scaled representations of spatial relations have been challenged by recognition of the inescapable imaginative and artistic content of cartographic processes and products that comes from framing, selection, composition and graphic representation of mapped information. This has opened up an exciting new field of connections between scientific map-making and creative art practices, apparent in the work of the individuals presented in this volume.

Third is the recognition of mapping as a complex cultural process in which the map itself is merely one stage. To understand the contents, meaning and significance of any map requires its reinsertion into the social and historical context from which it emerges and upon which it acts.

The following takes for granted these assumptions of a critical approach to the nature and history of maps, drawing on mapping history to highlight some of the continuities in maps and mapping practices that can easily become obscured by our excitement regarding the technical advances that have made 'mapping' such a dynamic contemporary field of practice and study.

A critical study of cartography can proceed from two directions: via study of the finished map, judging its function, technique, aesthetics and semiotics, or via study of mapping processes – both survey and compilation. From the first perspective we might consider Abraham Ortelius's 'Typus Orbis Terrarum' world map of 1570. Functionally, this provided the first modern atlas with an opening image of the terraqueous globe according to the most recent information available at the time of its making. The desire for empirical truth in the map is apparent from the changes made a mere seven years later when, among other improvements, the re-engraved map more accurately portrays the shape of South America. The selection of different colors for the continents anticipates the scale of representation for succeeding maps of the continents, in the ordered summary of geographical knowledge that constitutes the atlas.

Technically, the map adopts a modified cylindrical projection centered on the equator and a prime meridian running through the Azores, curving the meridians to meet at the poles. Like any projection of the sphere, this has distorting effects on shape and direction; in this case distortion is maximized towards the poles. Aesthetically, the map frames an oval planisphere with clouds that represent the element of air; the title is in clear typeface and the map makes effective use of color, shading, lettering and symbolization to provide a memorable and uncluttered image of lands and seas, an image to which subsequent maps in the atlas can be related. Aesthetics and science combine (but to our eyes undermine the accuracy of the map) in the balancing land masses north and south of the known continents – remnants of philosophical and religious belief in a harmonious distribution of lands over the surface of the earth.

The semiotics of the map are as complex as its scientific, technical and aesthetic aspects. The epigram at the base of the map (reinforced in the 1577 engraving by oculae at the corners) is taken from Cicero: 'For what can seem of moment in human affairs for him who keeps all eternity before his eyes and knows the scale of the universal world?' It indicates that the map has a greater role than that of scientific instrument and artistic image, reminding its viewer of the insignificance of human life compared to the vastness of creation. In presenting the 'theatre of the world' (to adopt the title of Ortelius's atlas) as a moral space, the map itself has an emblematic quality. This moral aspect of mapping can be traced back to the Mappa Mundi of the medieval Christian world and is also found in non-Western cartographic traditions . As we shall see, it has never disappeared from cartographic culture.

The alternative approach to a critical understanding of the cartographic image is via examination of survey and compilation, and these will be the focus here. 'Survey' means the direct collection and production of spatial data to be mapped

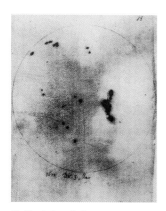

Galileo's 'map' of sunspots burned directly by the telescopic lens (1610).

(both the geodetic measure to create a base map and the informational content to be represented within its borders). Survey, or reconnaissance, has traditionally been a field-based activity within which instrumentation has played a formative role. 'Compilation' here means the gathering of survey information at a single place and its technical transformation into the finished map object.

This latter approach privileges the process of mapping over the product – the map – and it has attracted increasing attention in recent years, especially as it impacts upon the knowledge claims that might be made of the resulting map. Of particular concern have been the processes whereby knowledge gained in the field is transferred back to the place of compilation and whereby the map itself enters recursively into circuits of knowledge that generate further mappings. Mapping is itself a spatial process that involves negotiating problems of securing and maintaining the integrity of cartographic data as they move over space.

Turning first to survey, this is an embodied process involving sensual contact with the spaces to be mapped, above all by eye, as the word itself implies (from: *sur-voir*), although other senses can be critical in specific mapping situations, such as the cave where bodily touch is more significant than sight. In Western mapping since the Renaissance there has been a progressive shift away from trusting the human body as a reliable agent for recording spatial information towards dependence upon instrumentation as the guarantor of the accuracy and objectivity of survey data. This is first apparent in the use of the compass, astrolabe and cross-staff as aids to the human eye.

Optical instruments not only extend the scope of human vision but historically have been used to supplant it. Thus Galileo's revolutionary mappings of movement and imperfection in celestial space were founded on the capacity of the telescope lens not only to reveal the surface corrugations of the moon (traced directly onto paper by Galileo's hand), but to allow the sun to burn its dark spots onto the paper with no human intervention whatsoever.

The eighteenth century saw the radical extension of instrumentation to all aspects of survey or reconnaissance, using the alidade and plane table to operationalize techniques of triangulation that had been theorized as early as the mid-sixteenth century by Gemma Frisius, the mercury barometer to measure altitude and, most dramatically, for the mapping of oceanic space John Harrison's 1780s invention of the chronometer which allowed for the first time the easy and accurate measurement of longitude at sea.

But despite increased reliance on instrumentally measured survey, the human eye has remained the most critical element of mapping and the use of maps. Even with the chronometer, the British Admiralty long required all its officers, including the most junior, to learn sketching as a means for gathering and recording information about coastlines and harbors, considering drawing to be superior to any written account. Sketches were of two types: the memorial sketch, 'a delineation of a harbor, or any part of a coast, from the memory only, without notes or any immediate sight', conveying 'the general area of a bay, harbor, or island … shewing that some such places are there', and the eye-sketch, 'done by the eye at one station, without measuring distances; and drawn according to the apparent shape and dimensions of the land'.[1]

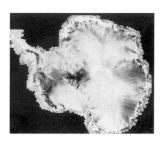

The first complete image of Antartica, imaged from space (NASA/Canadian Space Agency, 2000).

The teaching of these skills continued into the twentieth century. Invention of photography and of balloon then powered flight furthered the displacement of the human eye in geographic and topographic mapping. In 1915 Oskar Messter invented an airborne automatic camera that could film a 2.4-kilometer by 60-kilometer strip of earth surface in a sequence of overlapping frames that could be either printed as such or used as raw visual data.

Aerial photography replaced to some degree the heroic mapping expeditions of a Cassini or an Everest, surveying great arcs of meridian (from Dunkirk to Perpignan or Bangalore to Delhi). Photogrammetric survey was used in mapping great colonial stretches of Africa, Australia and Antarctica into the 1950s. But even aerial photography and its contemporary successor, remote-sensed imaging from orbiting satellites far above the earth's surface, have not wholly replaced the sensing human body. 'Ground truthing' was crucial for removing the errors caused for the 1950s British Antarctic Survey by magnetic deviation, cloud cover and distance distortions in polar regions. It remains necessary to ensure the instrumental accuracy of remote-sensed maps today.

In the mapping process, the supposed accuracy of survey secured by the replacement of the sensing but subjective human body by instruments is always threatened by the problems of transferring observed knowledge from the place of survey to the place of compilation. The sketch map can play a role in this but as the name suggests it lacks the authority of the 'true' surveyed map. The issue of securing the accuracy of mobile knowledge is beautifully expressed in *Le Petit Prince* by the French writer Antoine de St Exupery, who had himself been involved in aerial surveys of the French North African colonies. The Little Prince flies from planet to planet absorbing moral lessons from their inhabitants and discovering the strange habits of the adult world. The most beautiful of all the planets he visits is occupied by an old man, seated at a desk inscribing information into a great book. He is a geographer yet claims never to have seen the beauty of his planet. Bemused, the Little Prince asks why this is so.

The geographer is not the one who counts the towns, rivers, mountains, seas, oceans and deserts. The geographer is much too important to go wandering about. He never leaves his study. But he receives explorers. He interrogates them and notes their records. And if the records of a particular explorer seem interesting the geographer makes an enquiry into the moral character of that explorer.

Why is this so? Because a lying explorer would have catastrophic consequences for geography books (read maps). The same is true for an explorer who is a drunkard. How come?, enquires the Little Prince. Because drunkards see double. So the geographer would note down two mountains where only one exists.[2]

We shall return to this question of securing the truth of survey knowledge as it travels over space later on.

Recorded instrumentation and learned sketching techniques have been used to overcome the subjectivity of embodied observation but its removal is never complete. Cartographic instruments themselves have to be tested and calibrated: James Cook's Pacific navigation was partly intended to test the Harrison chronometer, the time-keeping instrument that finally permitted measurement of longitude at sea with reasonable speed and accuracy. During the seven-year survey by Pierre Méhain and Jean-Baptiste Delambre, begun in 1792 to calculate the precise length of an arc of meridian in order to establish the length of the meter as a universal measure (determined objectively as 1/40 millionth of the earth's polar circumference), 'every page of the expedition's record was signed by each member of the expedition or by outside witnesses to certify that the recorded measurements had been performed as described. No subsequent changes were permitted … the signatures radically transformed the status of the document'.[3]

Compilation brings its own interruptions to the apparently smooth transfer of spatial information from the territory to the map. Traditionally, the history of cartographic design was one of progressive movement from the pictorial style that we associate above all with baroque maps to unornamented graphic representation, the 'plain style' of the eighteenth and nineteenth centuries, a transition from art to science. Evidence was to be found in the changing appearance of maps themselves: the progressive removal of cartouches, elaborate lettering, naturalistic symbolization and the promiscuous inclusion of disconnected items of information.

In replacing such elements we observe the application of graticule and grid as controlling spatial metric and frame for the map, the substitution of measured contours and spot heights for hachures and relief shading to indicate topographic relief, the replacement at the map's margins of decorative framing devices by mathematical and statistical information (compass bearings and geodetic information, dates of survey and publication, scale etc) and the insertion of a key, explaining and controlling the use of color and symbolization. All these were intended as much to demonstrate the scientific credentials of the map's compilation as to provide for functional uses of the map. But we know that many such compilation decisions are inevitably arbitrary or driven by quite other than scientific considerations.

Clark's 1822 plain style map shows the distribution not only of religion but of 'civilization'. Less ideologically, why should water be colored blue, lowlands green or roads red? Why does the United States Geological Survey (USGS) topographic map

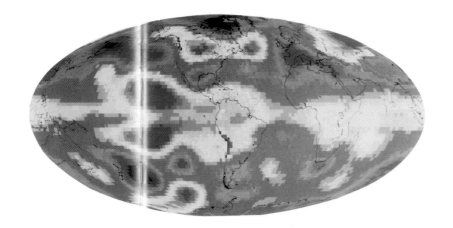

El Niño effect: satellite mosaic map of surface temperature variations (NASA, 1990).

mark schools but not the religious denomination of cemeteries indicated in the French Institut Geographique National (IGN) maps? Why do British Ordnance Survey (OS) maps mark and differentiate archeological sites by Roman and Gothic lettering? Even the remote-sensed image is a product of coloring choices applied by the map-maker to pixels received by the cartographic studio in numerical, digitized form. The powerful effect of the 1997 map of ocean temperatures that made graphically compelling the phenomenon of El Niño is the product of dramatic selection of color.

The intimate relations between mapping and science were initially forged in the late eighteenth and early nineteenth centuries. Enlightenment passion for universal measure and objective precision found expression in statistics, and statistics had their greatest social impact through graphic expression – graphs, charts and maps. The thematic map is an invention of this time. Alexander von Humboldt is credited with producing, in 1817, the first isoline map, a theoretical geographic surface rendered visible by connecting empirically observed points of equal value, the contour being the most familiar, although William Playfair had earlier pioneered 'lineal arithmetic'.

Humboldt's map showed variations in temperature across the Atlantic hemisphere, visually demonstrating the inadequacy of the Aristotelian model of climates. The shaded, or choropleth map, which uses territorial boundaries as containers for scaled statistical observations, replaced the tradition of recording numbers directly onto the map in the early 1800s, and by mid-century commanded widespread respect as a vehicle for demonstrating causal connections between spatially correlated phenomena. While the topographic map represents the specificity and uniqueness of places, the thematic map is 'a tool for nomothetic thinking' and thus for social planning. Dot maps, for example, were especially popular among medical doctors committed to the neo-hippocratic thesis of environmental causes for disease that was popular until Pasteur's work refocused attention on internal and biological causes.

The authority of thematic mapping derived from the statistical foundations of the information it conveyed. Given that such maps are generally produced by agencies for the better management of local territories, the problems of transporting knowledge are not as great as they are with exploratory geographic or topographic mapping. But thematic mapping suffers two fundamental and often unacknowledged weaknesses beyond the obvious methodological problems of interval and scaling choices.

First, the spatial correlations that such maps suggest are too readily interpreted as causal – what is called the 'ecological fallacy'. A telling example of this, deeply ironic in light of today's obsession with the health qualities of a 'Mediterranean diet', is the 1840 'Carte de la France Hernieuse' (Hernia map of France). This illustrated the incidence of hernias among the population of France by *département*. Six shading intervals were used to indicate the total number per 'hernious' individual within each *département*. Boundaries of other phenomena were then mapped across the data in order to reveal possible correlations with the incidence of hernia. One of the strongest correlations to which the compiler (a medical surgeon) drew attention was 'the northern limit of the olive tree', thus demonstrating cartographically the medical hypothesis that consumption of olive oil was a cause of hernia!

The second weakness of the choropleth map is iconographic: the choice of color shading to illustrate interval differences. The concept of 'shading' itself carries powerful moral connotations, and this was especially true in an era of self-conscious 'enlightenment' when darkness and shadow implied ignorance and decay – both physical and moral. Thus Edward Quinn's 1830 'Historical Atlas' used a similar device to Abraham Ortelius's parting clouds to surround his images of the earth, though in Quinn's case this reveals the darkness of ignorance being pushed progressively aside by the onward march of civilization through the ages.

On nineteenth-century thematic maps, color shading consistently used darkness to register failure in a spatial narrative of progress, thus French statistical cartography throughout the nineteenth century, in maps of educational standards, poverty and social provision, regularly divided the country into two parts: an 'enlightened' north where lighter shades dominated and an 'obscure' France south of a line from San Malo to Geneva, the failures of which were made visible through a cartographic gloom. A similar use of shading and the ecological fallacy is found on what today appear as extraordinary choropleth maps connecting the distribution of 'climatic energy' to that of 'civilization'.

If statistical mapping lost favor among medical researchers in the later nineteenth century, its popularity among social planners and 'hygienists' peaked in the early years of the twentieth century, as the 'civilization' maps suggest. Statistical survey and mapping of 'cultural traits' such as language, dialect and customs were central to debates between supporters of *Volk* and nation in determining the territorial extent of the unifying German Reich in the 1850s and 1860s. From the work of European social statisticians and statistical cartographers such as Frederick Le Play in France, Henry Mayhew in Britain, Heinrich Berghaus and American geological and soil surveyors such as John Wesley Powell or Eugene W Hilgard, emerged the idea of mapping as a critical tool of state policy as the concept of the 'survey' was transferred from the exploration of distant lands to hidden features of metropolitan societies. In the minds of social philosophers such as Patrick Geddes, a unified

Land use in the London area (Land Utilization Survey of Britain, 1937).

survey of the physical and social characteristics of a region could provide an ecological portrait of community in place and a stimulus to civic virtue and participation.

The survey did not require exploration over space but a kind of archeology of levels of interconnected relations in place, revealed by the very process of mapping. Such mapping would at best be the work of the community itself, working under instruction, in the process contributing to the further consolidation of civic virtues. Public display of the resulting maps would further this goal. Thus in the United States, where the commercial tradition of land mapping is in marked distinction to Europe's statist cadastral tradition, various states and counties in the 1920s, especially in New England and the Midwest farm states, encouraged schoolchildren to participate in local surveys that would reveal the true state of their community, particularly regarding its physical and moral health. Such maps had the effect of moral self-regulation, as in the example of a Springfield, Massachusetts survey map that flashed 1250 colored lights indicating the distribution of babies born in 1913: green for homes where the birth was registered, red for unregistered births (presumably out of wedlock).

In Britain, the survey movement peaked in the 1930s with the recruitment of schoolchildren from across England and Wales to map the use of every parcel of land, returning the results to London where they were compiled onto topographic base maps and colored to reveal national patterns of land use. Deep reds and purples dramatically revealed the octopus sprawl of great cities such as London, the suburban anonymity of which was supposedly threatening the civic virtues of more modest communities.

The moral fervor of survey mapping slowly declined after 1950 as the weaknesses of Modernist social engineering, which depended so heavily on statistical survey and mapping and which used the 'plan' – often in map form – as a central instrument of policy, became increasingly apparent. The late 1960s and early 1970s, which witnessed the crisis of comprehensive spatial planning, saw the convergence of the topographic map, the aerial photograph and the thematic map into a single form in the shape of the satellite image, later enhanced by the computer and GIS. These images have enormous graphic power, reshaping our vision and

Terrain image of Maat Mons, Venus (NASA, Magellan, 1994).

understanding of the world and our capacity to intervene in its material and social processes. Combined with the capacity to transmit data instantaneously and manipulate it on the computer screen, we have hugely increased the cartographic illusion of vision and action at a distance (the magic of maps). But we need to remain as alert as ever to the persuasive power of these newer cartographic images.

The widely reproduced image of 'Spaceship Earth' that dates from the last *Apollo* lunar mission of 1972 (the unique image of an unshadowed earth photographed by a human eye-witness) has too often been read uncritically as a sign of a vulnerable globe threatened by anthropogenic environmental crisis – a moral mapping of the treatment by humans of a nurturing Mother Earth. The image itself shows no evidence to support such a claim.

The story of how the whole-earth image was obtained by the *Apollo* astronauts, returned to earth, circulated globally and then interpreted, gaining agency in the discourses of environmentalism and one-world globalization, exemplifies many of the continuities in mapping as a spatial process.

Today, planets are being mapped without any human presence, data being returned to earth and translated into shapes and colors entirely by mechanical methods. In his work on the spatialities of scientific knowledge, the French historian of science Bruno Latour has used the term 'immutable mobile' to characterize those material agents that permit scientific discourse to sustain its claims of empirical warranty and repeatable truth in the absence of eye-witness evidence. The map appears at first sight as a perfect exemplar of the immutable mobile – a container of information gathered at specific locations, returned to a 'center of calculation' and then placed once more into circulation as a vehicle and instrument of scientific knowledge and further enquiry. The entire history of cartography can be told as a history of the struggle to realize such a status for the map. Thus Claudius Ptolemy (whose tables of locational coordinates for the Classical known world introduced modern mapping to Renaissance Europe) may never have drawn actual maps. His text provides the information necessary to construct a projection, and the coordinates necessary to produce the map. Text and tabulated figures are far more easily and accurately copied and transported than is a set of drawn maps.

Securing the immutability of the mobile has been a constant obsession of cartography, as we have seen. It is fundamental to the map's claim to be more than an imaginative picture. Cartographers have actually drawn upon the authority of cartographic procedure to grant legitimacy to complete fabrications. The sixteenth-century French cosmographer André Thevet, for example, placed measures of latitude and longitude around his maps of completely illusory islands. Such charlatanry reveals the ultimate impossibility of the cartographic conceit. The only true map is the territory itself, as pointed out long ago by Louis Borges.

The search to secure immutable mobility for the map reveals another Latourian feature – the prosthetic quality of cartography. The map is one of those instruments that serves to extend the capacities of the human body; it is a hybrid object, neither purely nature nor purely culture. Like the telescope or microscope, it allows us to see at scales impossible for the naked eye and without moving the physical body over space. The thematic map allows us to know of the presence of phenomena that are beyond our normal bodily senses, for example a trend surface map of property values or of air pollution. The map has a powerful recursive quality; it acts as a memory device that is also the basis for projective action. This is immediately apparent in the European mapping of discovery where the map is at once a necessary starting point for the exploration process and a principal outcome of that process.

These prosthetic and circulatory aspects of mapping are true also for the social survey and they remain so for the most technically advanced mappings of today. It is these features of the mapping process that make it such a fertile and powerful epistemology in knowing and representing the world. The map is at once empirically rooted and imaginatively liberated and liberating. Ultimately, all spaces are impossible to control, inhabit or represent completely. The map permits that illusion. It is a creative process of inserting our humanity into the world and seizing the world for ourselves. This is why the boundaries between the art and science of mapping, so long and so arbitrarily surveyed, charted and policed, are today smudged and fading, and why the imaginative and projective potential of mapping has become so vitally present in our lives.

Notes
1 Cited in Luciana Martins, 'Mapping tropical waters:British views and visions of Rio de Janeiro', in D Cosgrove (ed) *Mappings*, Reaktion Books (London), 1999, p 154.
2 Cited in Christian Jacobs, 'Mapping in the mind: the earth from ancient Alexandria', in Cosgrove, op cit, p 25.
3 Denis Guedj, *The Measure of the World*, trans Arthur Goldhammer, University of Chicago Press, 2001.

CONTRIBUTOR BIOGRAPHIES

Diana Balmori

founded landscape and urban design firm Balmori Associates Inc in 1990. Her work is particularly geared to the design of urban public space. She teaches at the Yale School of Architecture and at the Yale School of the Environment, and has brought about courses joining the two. Her projects have been exhibited in the Museum of Contemporary Art (Los Angeles), the Seventh Floor Gallery (New York City), Yale School of Architecture and Bard College.

Justine Cooper

has created self-portraits of her interior anatomy using computers and a magnetic resonance imaging (MRI) scanner. She displays these maps both as sculptures made with staked sheets of MRI film, and as video animations, which allow us to move through the body in time. She has exhibited widely throughout North America, Asia, Europe and Australia. Her work is currently held in collections in Australia, Europe and New York, including at the Metropolitan Museum of Art, Powerhouse Museum, Australian Center for the Moving Image, Griffith Artworks and the Queensland Art Gallery. She has lectured at the University of New South Wales, University of Western Sydney, University of Technology Sydney and the Sydney College of the Arts.

Denis Cosgrove

is the Alexander von Humboldt Professor of Geography at UCLA. He studies the relationship between advanced mapping techniques and their historical precedents, as well as mapping and the visual arts in geography, meaning and symbolism in landscape with specific reference to Italy and Western Europe, and Renaissance cosmography and the representation of the globe in European culture. He has published seven books, the most recent of which is *Apollo's Eye: A Cartographic Genealogy of the Earth in the Western Imagination* (2001).

Duane Dopkin

is a member of Paradigm Geo. As part of the company's below-ground visualization team he has been involved in the search for new oil sources using digitized seismic data specially displayed and analyzed in immersive 3-D environments.

Julie Dorsey

is a professor of computer science at Yale University, where she teaches computer graphics. Before joining the Yale faculty, she was a member at MIT. She received under-graduate degrees in architecture (BS and BArch 1987) and graduate degrees in computer science (MS 1990 and PhD 1993) from Cornell University. Her research interests include photorealistic image synthesis, material and texture models, illustration techniques and interactive visualization of complex scenes. In addition to serving on numerous conference program committees, she is an associate editor for IEEE *Transactions on Visualization and Computer Graphics* and *The Visual Computer*. She has received several professional awards, including MIT's Edgerton Faculty Achievement Award, a National Science Foundation Career Award, and an Alfred P Sloan Foundation Research Fellowship.

James Glymph

instituted the automated structural design (CATIA) and 3-D scanning system used in the offices of Frank Gehry Associates. This system has been applied to projects such as the Guggenheim Museum in Bilbao, Spain, as a way of translating physical models into computer data. His paradigm of mapping is based on the ability to faith-fully capture the subtle gestures and complex organiz-ations of Gehry's handcrafted models.

Eric Heller

maps the flow of electrons passing over bumpy surfaces.
Using extremely sensitive probes Heller can track up to 60,000 electron pathways in a single image. Images like 'Transport II' or 'Exponential' are generated with thousands of data points obtained from samples no larger than a typical bacterium. Heller is a professor of chemistry and a professor of physics at Harvard University.

Branden Hookway

is author of *Pandemonium: The Rise of Predatory Locales in the Postwar World* (1999). He is currently a PhD candidate in architecture theory at Princeton University. He has collaborated with Sanford Kwinter, Lars Lerup and Bruce Mau in the City-War Collective convened at Rice University in 1994.

Alicia Imperiale

is an artist, architect and critic based in New York City. She is assistant professor of architecture at Columbia University and Pratt Institute. She taught for Cornell University in Rome in the 2001 academic year, and received her Bachelor of Architecture from Pratt Institute and a Master of Fine Arts in Combined Media from Hunter College of the City University of New York. She has earned honors in numerous competitions, notably the Young Architects Forum of the Architectural League of New York, and the Van Alen Fellowship at the American Academy in Rome. Her work has focused on the links between art and architecture. In 1998 she co-curated a traveling exhibit on young American architects – 'architecture @ the edge'. Her research over the last few years has concentrated on the impact of digital technologies on art, architecture and architectural representation. This research is presented in her recent book, *New Flatness: Surface Tension in Digital Architecture* (2000). She has an essay on 'Digital skins: architecture of surface' in Ellen Lupton's *SKIN: Surface, Substance and Design* (2002), and has recently given talks on this subject at the ARCHILAB 2002 in Orleans, France; ETH of Zurich; the Polytechnic of Milan; John Cabot University in Rome; and the University of Louisiana, Baton Rouge. She was a panelist in connection with the exhibit 'Perfect Acts of Architecture' at the Heinz Architectural Center of the Carnegie Museum of Art, Pittsburgh. Forthcoming publications include 'Smooth Bodies' in the *Journal of Architectural Education*, and 'Fluid Alliances: Architecture, Politics and Fetish Post 9/11' will be published in the proceedings of the ARCHILAB conference by Thames and Hudson. She has shown her sculptural and multimedia works at the ONYX Showroom, Rome; HERE Gallery, New York City; and Foro Boario, Rome among others. Her work can be found at: *http://brooklyn.arch.columbia.edu/at_the_edge/ROME2000/architects/imperiale*.

Evan Jones

is assistant professor of music theory in the School of Music at Florida State University. He holds a PhD in music theory and a DMA in cello performance from the Eastman School of Music. While at Eastman, he coordinated and instructed a wide variety of music theory and aural skills courses; he also taught music theory at the University of Rochester and taught cello at Colgate University. At Florida State he teaches courses in sixteenth-century counterpoint, post-tonal aural skills and readings in music theory. He is a past winner of a Sproull Fellowship from the University of Rochester and a Doctoral Fellowship from the Social Sciences and Humanities Research Council of Canada, as well as teaching prizes from both Eastman and the University of Rochester. He has presented his research at numerous regional and national conferences, and has been published in *Perspectives of New Music and Computer Music Journal.* He has performed in Weill Recital Hall and Merkin Hall, among other venues, and previously served as co-editor of *Intégral*, a peer-reviewed journal of music theory. His dissertation and related papers focus on issues of voice leading in diatonic space; other research interests include the music of Iannis Xenakis, twentieth-century rhythm and meter, and the interaction of analysis and performance.

Paul Kaiser

and Shelley Eshkar received an award from the Foundation for Contemporary Performance Arts in 1998 and were fellows at the Cooper Union in 1997 and artists-in-residence at the Massachusetts Museum of Contemporary Art in 1999. Kaiser received his BA from Wesleyan University in 1978, where he was summa cum laude and a Phi Beta Kappa, and his Master of Education (MEd) in special education from the American University in 1983. His early work was in experimental film-making and performance audio tapes. He later spent ten years teaching students with severe learning disabilities, with whom he collaborated on making multimedia depictions of their own minds. This work earned him a Computer World/Smithsonian Award in 1991. In 1994, he moved to New York to create digital art. In 1996, he became the first interactive artist to receive a John Simon Guggenheim Memorial Foundation Fellowship, and in 2000 he was awarded a fellowship from the Brooklyn Academy of Music and Lucent. From 1996–98 he was a visiting lecturer at the Multimedia Studios
Program of San Francisco State University. He currently teaches a class in virtual film-making at Wesleyan University. Eshkar is a multimedia artist and experimental animator who began collaborating with Kaiser in 1995. He received a BFA from the Cooper Union School of Art in 1993, pursuing a multidisciplinary fine arts education. His innovations in 3-D figural drawing and animation have aroused considerable attention in the fields of computer graphics, dance and architecture. He has lectured to such diverse groups as SIGGRAPH, the East Coast Digital Consortium, the Congress of Research in Dance, Jacob's Pillow Dance Festival, Berkeley's CalPerformances, the Brooklyn Academy of Music and Harvard University's Graduate School of Design.

Takeo Kanade

received his PhD in electrical engineering from Kyoto University, Japan, in 1974. After being on the faculty of the Department of Information Science, Kyoto University, he joined the Computer Science Department and Robotics Institute in 1980. He became an associate professor in 1982, a full professor in 1985, the UA and Helen Whitaker Professor in 1993, and a university professor in 1998. He was the director of the Robotics Institute from 1992 to 2001, and served as the founding chairman (1989–93) of the Robotics PhD Program at CMU, probably the first of its kind in the world. He has worked in many areas of robotics, including manipulators, sensors, computer vision, multimedia applications and autonomous robots, and has published more than 200 papers on these topics. He was also the founding editor of the *International Journal of Computer Vision*. His professional honors include: election to the National Academy of Engineering, a Fellow of IEEE, a Fellow of ACM, a Fellow of American Association of Artificial Intelligence, and several awards including C & C Award, the Joseph Engelberger Award, Yokogawa Prize, JARA Award, Otto Franc Award and Marr Prize Award.

Lilla LoCurto and Bill Outcault

are sculptors whose work explores the use of 3-D laser-scanning technology to map the body. Working with a customized mapping program, the artists have developed special techniques for generating complex unfoldings from scans of their own bodies. Recent exhibitions include the widely traveled solo exhibition 'selfportrait.map' which originated at the List Visual Art Center at MIT. They also have solo shows in New York at the

Frederieke Taylor Gallery, Fundacio Joan Miro, Barcelona, Spain and Carpenter Center at Harvard University. Their work has been included in such group exhibitions as 'Situated Realities' in Baltimore, 'Digital: Printmaking Now' in East Hampton, New York and 'Contemporaneou.s.' in Cornwall and Sunderland, UK. They have also held residencies at Maryland Institute College of Art, Baltimore, Colorado State University, and Carpenter Center for the Visual Arts, Harvard University.

Brian McGrath

has been a practicing architect licensed in New York State since 1985. His current work is an outgrowth of his project *Transparent Cities*, a folio published by SITES Books with support from NYSCA in 1996. Over the past seven years as an adjunct associate professor at Columbia University's Graduate School of Architecture, Planning and Preservation, he has integrated computer-aided design into the Masters of Urban Design curriculum. Additionally, he has integrated the introduction of the computer as a design tool in both the BFA and Master of Architecture programs at Parsons School of Design. His work in this vein has been exhibited in the Queens Museum's 'City Speculations' exhibition of

1996 and at Parsons School of Design in a solo exhibition called 'Urban Diaries' in 1997 (*www.columbia.edu/~bpm7*). He has just completed a Fulbright Senior Scholar Fellowship at Chulalongkorn University in Bangkok, Thailand, where he consulted on curricula and computer technologies for a new Master of Urban Design Program for the Faculty of Architecture. Exhibitions include: 'Vacant Lots, New Schools for New York'. Publications include *The Transparent City, Rome Exposed*, and *Towards a Unifying Principle in Architectural Education*. He obtained his BArch from Syracuse University and MArch from Princeton University.

Konrad Pearlman

is a marketing representative and planning consultant for IT Spatial in McLean, Virginia. Having worked with GIS as a city and strategic planning consultant for the Washington GIS Consortium and the DC City-Wide GIS Project, he is an expert on the new 3-D GIS system being used by the Federal Government in Washington DC. With this new system it is possible to test architectural designs in situ and analyze how they impact their surroundings. Components of this system can depict future changes in the flow of vehicular traffic, use patterns for public transportation systems and pedestrian access. In the 1970s and 1980s he served as the deputy chief of planning and research in the DC Department of Housing and Community Development. He has held teaching positions at George Washington University, Catholic University, Boston Architectural Center and the University of Pennsylvania.

Michael Silver

holds a Master of Building Design from Columbia University, and is both a LeFevré research fellow for the Knowlton School of Architecture in Columbus, Ohio, and the director of digital media at the Yale School of Architecture. He has written numerous articles on the relationship between technology and design, and is the author of *Pamphlet Architecture #19: Reading/Drawing/Building*. He also directs the Office of Research and Development, a multidisciplinary design laboratory formally established at the turn of the century. In collaboration with other studios the office has worked at a variety of scales and has extensive experience in the design of furnishings, consumer products, websites and buildings. The use of advanced computer modeling tools were early projects that launched the studio on its current trajectory. Today the Office of Research and Development continues pioneering research in the field of digital mapping and architectural design. Current work explores the links between advanced 3-D surveillance technology and the fabrication devices that transform this mapping data into physical objects and spaces. As an experimental collaborative the office is

deeply committed to the precise alignment of advanced technology, visionary consciousness, architectural theory, academic scholarship and the logistics of building production.

Mark Watkins

is a designer of websites and graphics for museums, artists and architects. He is a member of the Urban-Interface collective with Brian McGrath. His client list includes Alice Aycock, Diller+Scofidio Architects and The Skyscraper Museum. A few of the projects have led to exhibitions at the Queen's Museum ('City Speculations'), the Gray Art Gallery ('The Luminous Design World of Shiro Kurumata') and have been published in the pages of *Wired* and *The New Yorker*. He is an adjunct instructor in the Media Studies and Digital Design programs at Parsons School of Design. He obtained his BA from the University of Southern California and MArch from the Parsons School of Design.

John Ziegler

is the founder and acting director of Space Track Inc, a New York-based mapping firm that specializes in new GIS techniques. His interest in GIS developed out of experience in urban planning and architecture, and from his government work with natural-hazard mapping and emergency management programs. He is currently using GIS to collate, organize and display the massive amounts of data being generated from the site of the 11 September tragedy. He is a chartered member of the American Institute of Certified Planners, a registered architect in New York State, and an adjunct professor of planning at New York University.